GRADES
K-2

D1312303

...the Super Source®
Tangrams

Cuisenaire Company of America, Inc.
White Plains, NY

Cuisenaire extends its warmest thanks to the many teachers and students across the country who helped ensure the success of the Super Source® series by participating in the outlining, writing, and field testing of the materials.

Project Director: Judith Adams
Managing Editor: Doris Hirschhorn
Editorial Team: Patricia Kijak Anderson, Linda Dodge, John Nelson, Deborah J. Slade, Harriet Slonim
Field Test Coordinator: Laurie Verdeschi

Design Manager: Phyllis Aycock
Text Design: Amy Berger, Tracey Munz
Line Art and Production: Joan Lee, Fiona Santoianni
Cover Design: Michael Muldoon
Illustrations: Rebecca Thornburgh

...the Super Source®
Table of Contents

INTRODUCTION
   USING *THE SUPER SOURCE*™. 4
   EXPLORING TANGRAMS 9

STRANDS AND TOPICS 12

OVERVIEW OF THE LESSONS. 16

LESSONS
   Cover and Count 18
   Fences for Fields. 22
   Flying Flags. 26
   Half-Time Show. 30
   Making a Quilt. 34
   Mirror Magician 38
   Rectangle Race 42
   Sailing Along. 46
   Same and Different 50
   Secret Builder 54
   Shape Morpher. 58
   Shapes Within Shapes. 62
   Tan Designs. 66
   Tangram Force-Out 70
   Tangrams Make Cents 74
   The Great Triangle Coverup 78
   Triangles Big and Small 82
   What's My Rule? 86

BLACKLINE MASTERS
   Cover-and-Count Game Board 90
   Blank *Cover-and-Count* Game Board . . 91
   Nine-Patch Quilt 92
   Rectangle Race Game Board. 93
   Sailboat 94
   Large Tangram Triangles 95
   Tan Designs 96
   Tangram Force-Out Game Board. 97

   Tangram Toy Cat 98
   More Tangram Toys. 99
   Tangram Paper 100
   Small Tangram Triangles 101
   Tangram Pieces 102
   1-Centimeter Grid Paper 103
   Tangram Writing Paper 104

Using the Super Source™

The Super Source™ is a series of books, each of which contains a collection of activities to use with a specific math manipulative. Driving **the Super Source™** is Cuisenaire's conviction that children construct their own understandings through rich, hands-on mathematical experiences. Although the activities in each book are written for a specific grade range, they all connect to the core of mathematics learning that is important to every K-6 child. Thus, the material in many activities can easily be refocused for children at other grade levels. Because the activities are not arranged sequentially, children can work on any activity at any time.

The lessons in **the Super Source™** all follow a basic structure consistent with the vision of mathematics teaching described in the *Curriculum and Evaluation Standards for School Mathematics* published by the National Council of Teachers of Mathematics.

All of the activities in this series involve Problem Solving, Communication, Reasoning, and Mathematical Connections—the first four NCTM Standards. Each activity also focuses on one or more of the following curriculum strands: Number, Geometry, Measurement, Patterns/Functions, Probability/Statistics, Logic.

HOW LESSONS ARE ORGANIZED

At the beginning of each lesson, you will find, to the right of the title, both the major curriculum strands to which the lesson relates and the particular topics that children will work with. Each lesson has three main sections. The first, GETTING READY, offers an *Overview*, which states what children will be doing, and why, and provides a list of "What You'll Need." Specific numbers of Tangram pieces or entire sets are suggested on this list but can be adjusted as the needs of your specific situation dictate. Before the activity, Tangram pieces or sets can be counted out and placed in containers or self-sealing plastic bags for easy distribution. Blackline masters that are provided for your convenience at the back of the book are referenced on this materials list. Paper, pencils, scissors, tape, and materials for making charts, which may be necessary in some activities, are not.

Although overhead Tangram pieces and overhead Tangram recording paper are always listed in "What You'll Need" as optional, these materials are highly effective when you want children to see a demonstration using Tangrams. As you move the pieces on the screen, children can work with the same materials at their seats. Children can also use the overhead to present their work to other members of their group or to the class.

The second section, THE ACTIVITY, first presents a possible scenario for *Introducing* the children to the activity. The aim of this brief introduction is to help you give children the tools they will need to investigate independently. However, care has been taken to avoid undercutting the activity itself. Since these investigations are designed to enable children to increase their own mathematical power, the idea is to set the stage but not steal the show! The heart of the lesson, *On Their Own*, is found in a box at the top of the second page of each lesson. Here, rich problems stimulate many different problem-solving approaches and lead to a variety of solutions. These hands-on explorations have the potential for bringing children to new mathematical ideas and deepening skills.

On Their Own is intended as a stand-alone activity for children to explore with a partner or in a small group. Be sure to make the needed directions clearly visible. You may want to write them on the chalkboard or on an overhead or present them either on reusable cards or paper. For children who may have difficulty reading the directions, you can read them aloud or make sure that at least one "reader" is in each group.

The last part of this second section, *The Bigger Picture*, gives suggestions for how children can share their work and their thinking and make mathematical connections. Class charts and children's recorded work provide a springboard for discussion. Under "Thinking and Sharing," there are several prompts that you can use to promote discussion. Children will not be able to respond to these prompts with one-word answers. Instead, the prompts encourage children to describe what they notice, tell how they found their results, and give the reasoning behind their answers. Thus children learn to verify their own results rather than relying on the teacher to determine if an answer is "right" or "wrong." Though the class discussion might immediately follow the investigation, it is important not to cut the activity short by having a class discussion too soon.

The Bigger Picture often includes a suggestion for a "Writing" (or drawing) assignment. This is meant to help children process what they have just been doing. You might want to use these ideas as a focus for daily or weekly entries in a math journal that each child keeps.

From: _Mirror Magician_

From: _Shape Morpher_

The Bigger Picture always ends with ideas for "Extending the Activity." Extensions take the essence of the main activity and either alter or extend its parameters. These activities are well used with a class that becomes deeply involved in the primary activity or for children who finish before the others. In any case, it is probably a good idea to expose the entire class to the possibility of, and the results from, such extensions.

The third and final section of the lesson is TEACHER TALK. Here, in *Where's the Mathematics?*, you can gain insight into the underlying mathematics of the activity and discover some of the strategies children are apt to use as they work. Solutions are also given—when such are necessary and/or helpful. Because *Where's the Mathematics?* provides a view of what may happen in the lesson as well as the underlying mathematical potential that may grow out of it, this may be the section that you want to read before presenting the activity to children.

USING THE ACTIVITIES

The Super Source™ has been designed to fit into the variety of classroom environments in which it will be used. These range from a completely manipulative-based classroom to one in which manipulatives are just beginning to play a part. You may choose to use some activities in *the Super Source*™ in the way set forth in each lesson (introducing an activity to the whole class, then breaking the class up into groups that all work on the same task, and so forth). You will then be able to circulate among the groups as they work to observe and perhaps comment on each child's work. This approach requires a full classroom set of materials but allows you to concentrate on the variety of ways that children respond to a given activity.

Alternatively, you may wish to make two or three related activities available to different groups of children at the same time. You may even wish to use different manipulatives to explore the same mathematical concept. (Pattern Blocks and Geoboards, for example, can be used to teach some of the same geometric principles as Tangrams.) This approach does not require full classroom sets of a particular manipulative. It also permits greater adaptation of materials to individual children's needs and/or preferences.

If children are comfortable working independently, you might want to set up a "menu"— that is, set out a number of related activities from which children can choose. Children should be encouraged to write about their experiences with these independent activities.

However you choose to use *the Super Source*™ activities, it would be wise to allow time for several groups or the entire class to share their experiences. The dynamics of this type of interaction, where children share not only solutions and strategies but also feelings and intuitions, is the basis of continued mathematical growth. It allows children who are beginning to form a mathematical structure to clarify it and those who have mastered just isolated concepts to begin to see how these concepts might fit together.

Again, both the individual teaching style and combined learning styles of the children should dictate the specific method of utilizing *the Super Source*™ lessons. At first sight, some activities may appear too difficult for some of your children, and you may find yourself tempted to actually "teach" by modeling exactly how an activity can lead to a particular learning outcome. If you do this, you rob children of the chance to try the activity in whatever way they can. As long as children have a way to begin an investigation, give them time and opportunity to see it through. Instead of making assumptions about what children will or won't do, watch and listen. The excitement and challenge of the activity—as well as the chance to work cooperatively—may bring out abilities in children that will surprise you.

If you are convinced, however, that an activity does not suit your students, adjust it, by all means. You may want to change the language, either by simplifying it or by referring to specific vocabulary that you and your children already use and are comfortable with. On the other hand, if you suspect that an activity isn't challenging enough, you may want to read through the activity extensions for a variation that you can give children instead.

RECORDING

Although the direct process of working with Tangrams is a valuable one, it is afterward, when children look at, compare, share, and think about their constructions, that an activity yields its greatest rewards. However, because it is not always possible to leave Tangram constructions intact, children need an effective way to record their work and need to be encouraged to find ways to transfer their Tangram shapes. To this end, at the back of this book, Tangram paper is provided for reproduction, as are outlines of the Tangram pieces.

It is important that children use a method of recording that they feel comfortable with. Frustration in recording their shapes can leave children feeling that the actual activity was either too difficult or just not fun! Thus, recording methods that are appropriate for a specific class or for specific children might be suggested. For example, children might choose to trace each Tangram piece in their shape onto Tangram paper or onto plain paper, to cut out, color, and tape or paste down paper Tangram pieces, or to use a Tangram template to reproduce the pieces that make up their shapes. You can buy a TANplate, which includes all of the Tangram pieces, or you can make homemade templates by carefully cutting out each shape from a plastic coffee-can lid.

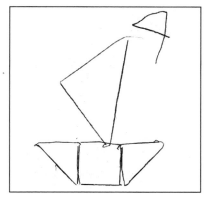

From: *Sailing Along*

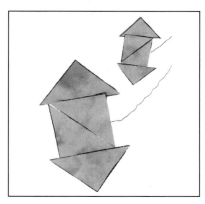

From: *Triangles Big and Small*

From: *Making a Quilt*

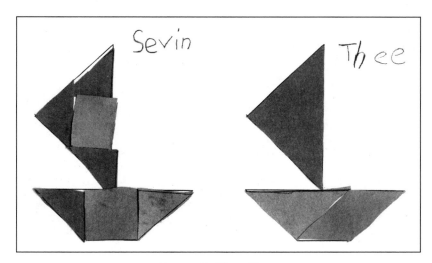

From: *Sailing Along*

Another interesting way to "freeze" a Tangram shape is to create it using a software piece, such as *Journey with Tangrams* or *Shape Up!*, and then get a printout. Children can use a classroom or resource room computer if it is available or, where possible, extend the activity into a home assignment by utilizing their home computers. Since both children and adults enjoy Tangram puzzles, Tangrams, whether "in hand" or "on screen," can prove very helpful in making the home-school connection.

For many Tangram activities, recording involves copying the placement of the Tangram pieces. Yet, since there is a natural progression from thinking with manipulatives to a verbal description of what was done to a written record of it, as children work through the Tangram activities they should also be encouraged to record their thinking processes. Writing, drawing, and making charts and tables are also ways to record. By creating a table of data gathered in the course of their investigations, children are able to draw conclusions and look for patterns. When children write or draw, either in their group or later by themselves, they are clarifying their understanding of their recent mathematical experience.

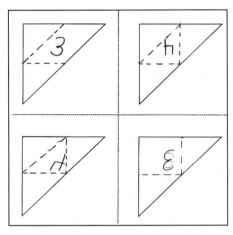

From: *Shapes Within Shapes*

From: *Cover and Count*

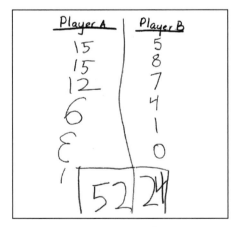

From: *Cover and Count*

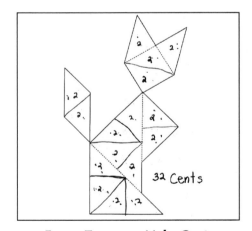

From: *Tangrams Make Cents*

With a roomful of children busily engaged in their investigations, it is not easy for a teacher to keep track of how individual children are working. Having tangible material to gather and examine when the time is right will help you to keep in close touch with each child's learning.

Exploring Tangrams

The Tangram is a deceptively simple set of seven geometric shapes made up of five triangles (two small triangles, one medium triangle, and two large triangles), a square, and a parallelogram. When the pieces are arranged together they suggest an amazing variety of forms, embodying many numerical and geometric concepts. The Tangram pieces are widely used to solve puzzles which require the making of a specified shape using all seven pieces. Cuisenaire's seven-piece plastic Tangram set comes in in four colors—red, green, blue, and yellow.

The three different-sized Tangram triangles are all similar, right isosceles triangles. Thus, the triangles all have angles of 45°, 45°, and 90°, and the corresponding sides of these triangles are in proportion.

Another interesting aspect of the Tangram set is that all of the Tangram pieces can be completely covered with small Tangram triangles.

small triangle	medium triangle	square	parallelogram	large triangle

Hence, it is easy to see that all the angles of the Tangram pieces are multiples of 45—that is, 45°, 90°, or 135°, and that the small Tangram triangle is the unit of measure that can be used to compare the areas of the Tangram pieces. Since the medium triangle, the square, and the parallelogram are each made up of two small Tangram triangles, they each have an area twice that of the small triangle. The large triangle is made up of four small Tangram triangles and thus has an area four times that of the small triangle and twice that of the other Tangram pieces.

Another special aspect of the pieces is that all seven fit together to form a square.

Some children can find the making of Tangram shapes to be very frustrating, especially if they are used to being able to "do" math by following rules and algorithms. For such children, you can reduce the level of frustration by providing some hints. For example, you can put down a first piece, or draw lines on an outline to show how pieces can be placed. However, it is important to find just the right level of challenge so that children can experience the pleasure of each Tangram investigation. Sometimes, placing some Tangram pieces incorrectly and then modeling an exploratory approach like the following may make children feel more comfortable: "I wonder if I could put this Tangram piece this way. I guess not, because then nothing else can fit here. So I'd better try another way...."

WORKING WITH TANGRAMS

Tangrams are a good tool for developing spatial reasoning and for exploring fractions and a variety of geometric concepts, including size, shape, congruence, similarity, area, perimeter, and the properties of polygons. Tangrams are especially suitable for children's independent work, since each child can be given a set for which he or she is responsible. However, since children vary greatly in their spatial abilities and language, some time should also be allowed for group work, and most children need ample time to experiment freely with Tangrams before they begin more serious investigations.

Young children will at first think of their Tangram shapes literally. With experience, they will see commonalities and begin to develop abstract language for aspects of patterns within their shapes. For example, children may at first make a square simply from two small triangles. Yet eventually they may develop an abstract mental image of a square divided by a diagonal into two triangles, which will enable them to build squares of other sizes from two triangles.

Tangrams can also provide a visual image essential for developing an understanding of fraction algorithms. Many children learn to do examples such as 1/2 = ?/8 or 1/4 + 1/8 + 1/16 = ? at a purely symbolic level so that if they forget the procedure, they are at a total loss. Children who have had many presymbolic experiences solving problems such as "Find how many small triangles fill the large triangles," or "How much of the full square is covered by a small, a medium, and a large triangle?" will have a solid intuitive foundation on which to build these basic skills and to fall back on if memory fails them.

Young children have an initial tendency to work with others, and to copy one another's work. Yet, even duplicating someone else's Tangram shape can expand a child's experience, develop the ability to recognize similarities and differences, and provide a context for developing language related to geometric ideas. Throughout their investigations, children should be encouraged to talk about their constructions in order to clarify and extend their thinking. For example, children will develop an intuitive feel for angles as they fit corners of Tangram pieces together, and they can be encouraged to think about why some will fit in a given space and others won't. Children can begin to develop a perception of symmetry as they take turns "mirroring" Tangram pieces across a line placed between them on a mat and can also begin to experience pride in their joint production.

Children of any age who haven't seen Tangrams before are likely to first explore shapes by building objects that look like objects—perhaps a butterfly, a rocket, a face, or a letter of the alphabet. Children with a richer geometric background are likely to impose interesting restrictions on their constructions, choosing to make, for example, a filled-in polygon, such as a square or hexagon, or a symmetric pattern.

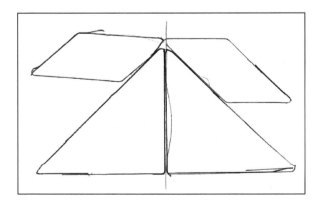

From: *Flying Flags*

From: *Half-Time Show*

ASSESSING CHILDREN'S UNDERSTANDING

The use of Tangrams provides a perfect opportunity for authentic assessment. Watching children work with the Tangram pieces gives you a visual sense of how they approach a mathematical problem. Their thinking can be "seen," in so far as that thinking is expressed through their positioning of the Tangram pieces, and when a class breaks up into small working groups, you are able to circulate, listen, and raise questions, all the while focusing on how individuals are thinking.

To ensure that children know not only how to do a certain operation but also how it relates to a model, assessment should include not only symbolic pencil-and-paper tasks such as "Find 1/2 + 1/8," but also performance tasks such as "Show why your answer is correct using Tangram pieces."

Having children describe their creations and share their strategies and thinking with the whole class gives you another opportunity for observational assessment. Furthermore, since spatial thinking plays an important role in children's intellectual development, include in your overall assessment some attention to spatial tasks.

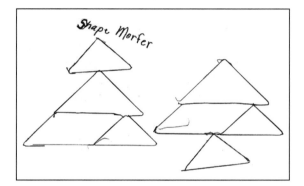

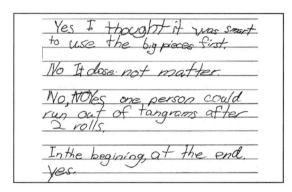

From: *Shape Morpher*

Models of teachers assessing children's understanding can be found in Cuisenaire's series of videotapes listed below.

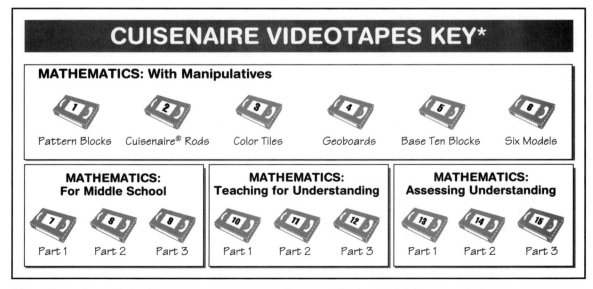

*See *Overview of the Lessons*, pages 16–17, for specific lesson/video correlation.

Connect
the Super Source™
to NCTM Standards.

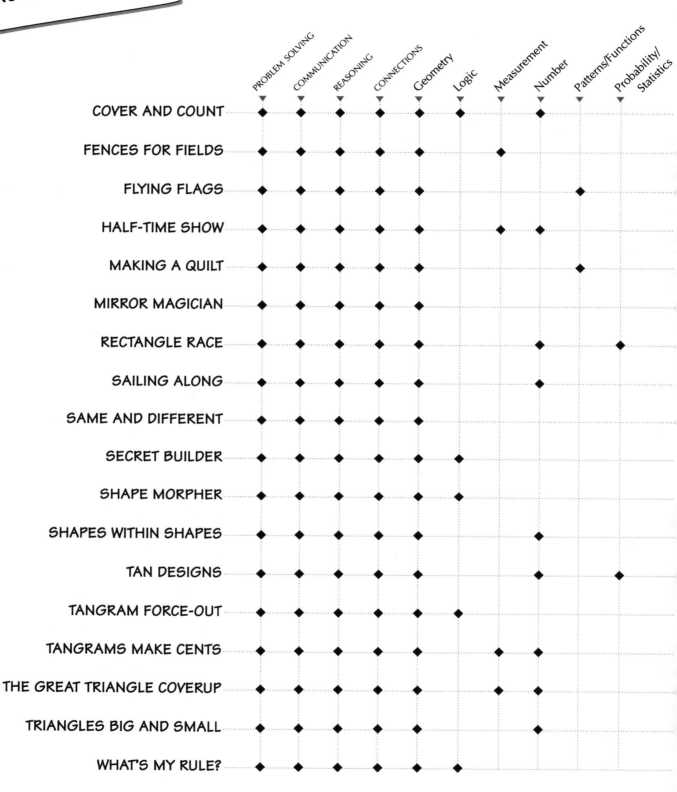

	PROBLEM SOLVING	COMMUNICATION	REASONING	CONNECTIONS	Geometry	Logic	Measurement	Number	Patterns/Functions	Probability/Statistics
COVER AND COUNT	◆	◆	◆	◆	◆	◆		◆		
FENCES FOR FIELDS	◆	◆		◆	◆		◆			
FLYING FLAGS	◆	◆		◆	◆				◆	
HALF-TIME SHOW	◆	◆		◆	◆			◆		
MAKING A QUILT	◆	◆		◆	◆				◆	
MIRROR MAGICIAN	◆	◆		◆	◆					
RECTANGLE RACE	◆	◆		◆	◆			◆		◆
SAILING ALONG	◆	◆		◆	◆			◆		
SAME AND DIFFERENT	◆	◆		◆	◆					
SECRET BUILDER	◆	◆	◆	◆	◆	◆				
SHAPE MORPHER	◆	◆	◆		◆					
SHAPES WITHIN SHAPES	◆	◆	◆	◆	◆			◆		
TAN DESIGNS	◆	◆	◆	◆	◆			◆		◆
TANGRAM FORCE-OUT	◆	◆	◆	◆	◆	◆				
TANGRAMS MAKE CENTS	◆	◆	◆	◆	◆		◆	◆		
THE GREAT TRIANGLE COVERUP	◆	◆	◆	◆	◆			◆	◆	
TRIANGLES BIG AND SMALL	◆	◆	◆	◆	◆			◆		
WHAT'S MY RULE?	◆	◆	◆	◆	◆	◆				

TOPICS

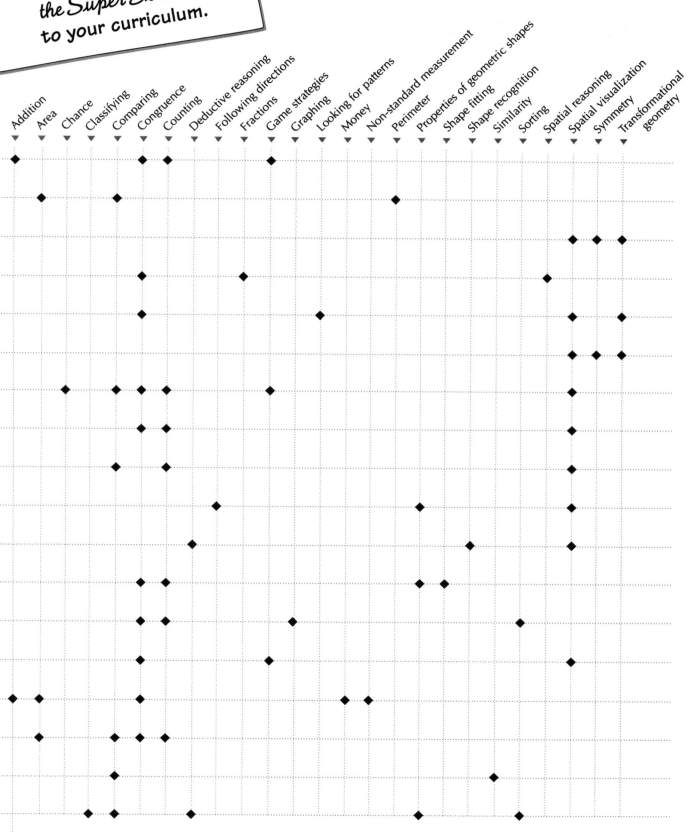

Addition · Area · Chance · Classifying · Comparing · Congruence · Counting · Deductive reasoning · Following directions · Fractions · Game strategies · Graphing · Looking for patterns · Money · Non-standard measurement · Perimeter · Properties of geometric shapes · Shape fitting · Shape recognition · Similarity · Sorting · Spatial reasoning · Spatial visualization · Symmetry · Transformational geometry

Classroom-tested activities contained in these *Super Source*™ Tangrams books focus on the math strands in the charts below.

...the Super Source™ **Tangrams, Grades 3-4**

Geometry	Logic	Measurement
Number	Patterns/Functions	Probability/Statistics

...the Super Source™ **Tangrams, Grades 5-6**

Geometry	Logic	Measurement
Number	Patterns/Functions	Probability/Statistics

More **SUPER SOURCE**™
at a glance:
ADDITIONAL MANIPULATIVES
for Grades K-2

Classroom-tested activities contained in these *Super Source*™ books focus on the math strands as indicated in these charts.

...the *Super Source*™ Snap™ Cubes, Grades K-2

Geometry	Logic	Measurement
Number	**Patterns/Functions**	**Probability/Statistics**

...the *Super Source*™ Cuisenaire® Rods, Grades K-2

Geometry	Logic	Measurement
Number	**Patterns/Functions**	**Probability/Statistics**

...the *Super Source*™ Geoboards, Grades K-2

Geometry	Logic	Measurement
Number	**Patterns/Functions**	**Probability/Statistics**

...the *Super Source*™ Color Tiles, Grades K-2

Geometry	Logic	Measurement
Number	**Patterns/Functions**	**Probability/Statistics**

...the *Super Source*™ Pattern Blocks, Grades K-2

Geometry	Logic	Measurement
Number	**Patterns/Functions**	**Probability/Statistics**

Overview of the Lessons

COVER AND COUNT **18**

Counting, Addition, Congruence, Game strategies

In this game for two players, children fit Tangram pieces on a dotted grid in an effort to cover as many dots as possible.

FENCES FOR FIELDS **22**

Perimeter, Comparing, Area

Children make a shape from four Tangram pieces, then find the distance around the shape.

FLYING FLAGS **26**

Symmetry, Spatial visualization, Transformational geometry

Children trace Tangram pieces along a vertical line, flip them, and trace them again to make a symmetrical match.

HALF-TIME SHOW **30**

Spatial reasoning, Fractions, Congruence

Children use two different colors of Tangram pieces to make a shape in which each colored section covers one half of the shape.

MAKING A QUILT **34**

 Spatial visualization, Looking for patterns, Transformational geometry, Congruence

Children make paper quilts based on quilt-square patterns they design using Tangram triangles.

MIRROR MAGICIAN **38**

Symmetry, Spatial visualization, Transformational geometry

In this game for two players, children build mirrored images of Tangram shapes in an effort to form patterns that have line symmetry.

RECTANGLE RACE **42**

Chance, Counting, Comparing, Congruence, Spatial visualization, Game strategies

In this game for two players, children take turns placing Tangram pieces on a game board according to a roll of a number cube in an effort to be the one to put down the last piece.

SAILING ALONG **46**

 Counting, Spatial visualization, Congruence

Children use Tangram pieces to fill in the outline of a sailboat, first using the least number, then the greatest number, of pieces possible.

SAME AND DIFFERENT **50**

Comparing, Counting, Spatial visualization

Children make shapes from four Tangram pieces of their own choosing. Then they compare their shapes, discussing how they are alike and how they are different.

 See video key, page 11.

Tangrams, Grades K-2

SECRET BUILDER 54

Spatial visualization, Properties of geometric shapes, Following directions

Children take turns making secret shapes from Tangram pieces. They describe their shapes to their partners, who try to make the shapes from the directions they are given.

SHAPE MORPHER 58

Spatial visualization, Shape recognition, Deductive reasoning

In this game for four or more players, children take turns being the Shape Morpher who creates and changes a shape using four Tangram pieces.

SHAPES WITHIN SHAPES 62

Shape Fitting, Counting, Properties of geometric shapes, Congruence

Children explore different ways to fill an outline of the large Tangram triangle with other Tangram pieces.

TAN DESIGNS 66

Sorting, Counting, Graphing, Congruence

Children fill a rectangular outline with Tangram pieces, then record the pieces and the number of each kind of piece they used.

TANGRAM FORCE-OUT 70

Spatial visualization, Congruence, Game strategies

In this game for two players, children take turns placing Tangram pieces on a grid in an effort to be the one to put down the last piece.

TANGRAMS MAKE CENTS 74

Addition, Money, Congruence, Non-standard measurement, Area

Using an assigned monetary value for the small Tangram triangle, children find the cost of "toys" made up of Tangram pieces.

THE GREAT TRIANGLE COVERUP 78

Counting, Comparing, Area, Congruence

Children make a shape by joining two Tangram pieces. Then they count the number of small triangles needed to cover their new shape.

TRIANGLES BIG AND SMALL 82

Comparing, Similarity

Children make shapes with four large Tangram triangles, then try to make the same shape with four small triangles

WHAT'S MY RULE? 86

Comparing, Classifying, Sorting, Properties of geometric shapes, Deductive reasoning

In this game for two to four players, children take turns making rules that identify certain Tangram pieces and guessing rules made by others.

See video key, page 11.

COVER AND COUNT

- Counting
- Addition
- Congruence
- Game strategies

Getting Ready

What You'll Need

Tangrams, 2 sets of 2 different colors per pair

Snap™ Cubes (optional)

Cover-and-Count game board, page 90

Blank *Cover-and-Count* game board, page 91

Die, 1 per pair

Overhead Tangram pieces and/or *Cover-and-Count* game board transparency (optional)

Overview

In this game for two players, children fit Tangram pieces on a dotted grid in an effort to cover as many dots as possible. In this activity, children have the opportunity to:

- ◆ develop an understanding of how Tangram shapes are related
- ◆ count groups of dots, find their sums, and compare the sums
- ◆ develop strategic thinking skills

The Activity

You many want to encourage some children to match Snap Cubes or other small counters one-to-one to the covered dots in each section. Children can then keep their Snap Cubes in trains of five or ten, later finding the sum of their dots by counting by fives or tens and adding any additional dots to the total.

Introducing

- ◆ Display the *Cover-and-Count* game board. Explain that children will use it to play a game in which they use Tangram pieces to cover as many dots as they can.
- ◆ Invite a child to place a large Tangram triangle anywhere on the game board. Tell the child that the piece must fit over the game board sections exactly.
- ◆ Point out that, when the large triangle is fitted properly on the board, it covers eight grid sections, and not nine.

Okay   Not okay

8 sections   9 sections

- ◆ Demonstrate how to lift one side of the piece to peek under it to see the dots in each covered section. Then count the dots and write the total number of covered dots on the chalkboard.
- ◆ Explain that in the upcoming game, the player who covers the greater number of dots will be the winner.

On Their Own

Play *Cover and Count!*

Here are the rules.

1. This is a game for 2 players. Each player needs a different colored Tangram set. The object is to use Tangram pieces to cover as many dots on a grid as possible.

2. Players take turns choosing a Tangram piece and fitting it on a game board that looks like this one. The Tangram piece must fit over the game board sections exactly.

Okay     Not okay

3. Players try to put down pieces to cover as many dots as they can. They write down the number of dots they cover on a turn.

4. The game ends when players run out of pieces or when there is no room for more pieces on the game board.

5. Each player finds the total number of dots that he or she covered. The winner is the one who covered the most dots.

- Play 3 games of *Cover and Count.*
- Be ready to talk about good moves and bad moves.

The Bigger Picture

Thinking and Sharing

Invite children to talk about their games and describe some of the thinking they did.

Use prompts such as these to promote class discussion:

- ◆ What can you do to cover a lot of dots in a game?
- ◆ At the beginning of a game, which Tangram pieces are the easiest to put down? Does this change as the game goes on? How?
- ◆ What can you do to keep your partner from covering a lot of dots?
- ◆ How did you keep track of your dots? Was this a good way? Why?
- ◆ Did you ever work with your partner and as a team try to cover up all the dots? Were you able to cover them all?

Extending the Activity

1. Have children play the game again, except this time, make the winner the child who covers the least number of dots.

2. Distribute blank *Cover-and-Count* game boards. Have each child fill in a number of dots (from 1 to 6) in many of the grid sections. Encourage pairs to play the game again on each of these new game boards.

Teacher Talk

Where's the Mathematics?

Cover and Count calls for the use of numerical, logical, and spatial strategies. In attempting to cover the most dots, children visualize where pieces could fit. Then they use this knowledge to plan future moves and deny their partner high-scoring moves.

In discussing their strategies, children may reveal that they use the largest Tangram pieces at the beginning of the game at which time there is more space available to place them. Toward the end of a game, fitting the remaining pieces into the available space by analyzing size and shape becomes the challenge.

As they play the game, children may discover that larger pieces can usually cover more dots than can the smaller pieces. Using the large triangle, children can cover up to 18 dots in one move.

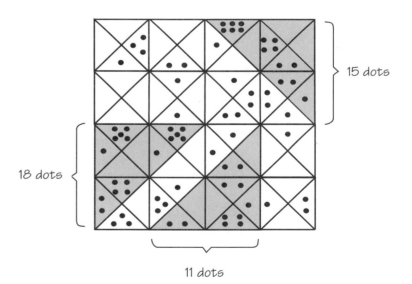

After children have played several games, they can disclose the strategies they developed for winning and for blocking their partners. Children may volunteer these strategies: placing large pieces early in the game, saving the small triangles until later in the game, and blocking by placing some pieces to limit spaces so that certain dots cannot be covered by either player.

3. To play a challenging variation of the game, have players take turns rolling a die and then choosing a Tangram piece that will cover the same number of dots as the number rolled. For example, the child who rolls a 5 should look for a Tangram piece that will cover a dot combination equal to five. Children may work alone, cooperatively, or against an opponent. If a piece cannot be placed to match a roll of the die, the player rolls again.

To determine the winner, children may use different ways of finding their total numbers of dots. Some may add the numbers written in columns; others may make a tally mark for each dot. Still others may decide to use Snap™ Cubes or some type of counter (Color Tiles, Tangrams, or beads) to represent the covered dots.

Partners may have different playing styles. Some children will play *Cover and Count* as a game of chance, whereas others will consider their moves more carefully, mentally exploring the consequences of the various placement of pieces.

As children explore different game strategies, they may become convinced that their strategy is best or that it will always work. You may want to have them test their ideas by assigning certain children to use a certain strategy. Discuss whether one strategy always wins. Ask what happens when two opponents use the same strategy.

Children may try to play the game cooperatively in an effort to cover all the dots. This can be done in several different ways. One such way is shown here:

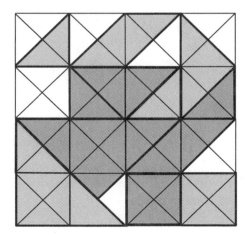

FENCES FOR FIELDS

Getting Ready

What You'll Need

Tangrams, 1 set per pair

Tape

Tangram paper, page 100

Scissors

Length of string, 20 small paper clips or pipe cleaners (2 or 3 twisted together at the ends) per pair

Overhead Tangram pieces and/or Tangram paper transparency (optional)

Overview

Children make a shape from four Tangram pieces, then find the distance around the shape. In this activity, children have the opportunity to:

◆ measure to find the perimeter of a shape

◆ develop the understanding that the same Tangram pieces can be used to form shapes with different perimeters

The Activity

Introducing

◆ Trace around a large Tangram triangle on the chalkboard to produce these shapes (or make them from paper Tangrams).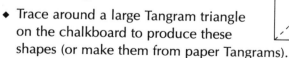

◆ Ask children whether or not the shapes are the same size. Have them explain their answer.

◆ Elicit that since the same two pieces were used for both shapes, both cover the same amount of space.

◆ Model for children how to measure around the edges of the shapes using a length of string for each (or any other flexible measuring tool).

◆ Compare the lengths of string. Elicit that one is longer than the other.

On Their Own

How can you find the fencing needed to go around a field?

- With a partner, put these 4 Tangram pieces together to make a field.

   Make sure the sides of the pieces line up exactly. Tape the pieces to hold the field together.
- Put your field on a piece of Tangram paper. Trace around the outside edges of it. Cut out your field.
- Find out how much fencing this field needs by using string to measure the distance around it. Cut the string to the right length.
- Tape one end of the fence, or string, to a bottom corner of your field.
- Use the same 4 pieces to make fields of different shapes. Repeat the process of finding the fencing for each.
- Be ready to compare your fields and fences.

The Bigger Picture

Thinking and Sharing

Draw a horizontal line across the chalkboard. Invite a pair to tape their fields on the line so that one end of the string touches the line and the rest hangs below the line. Continue until all fields and strings are displayed across the board.

Use prompts such as these to promote class discussion:

- What do you notice about the posted fields?
- What do you notice about the lengths of the strings? Why did this happen?
- Which field needs the least fencing? How do you know?
- Would the field that has the longest string hold more cows than the other fields? Explain.
- What other ways can you think of to measure around a field?

Drawing

Tell children to choose one of the posted fields and draw it the way it might look on a farm. Have them glue a piece of string around the field on their papers to make a fence. Suggest that they draw some animals inside the fence.

1. Repeat the activity, this time having children measure the distance around their fences using the short side of a small Tangram triangle.

Teacher Talk

Where's the Mathematics?

This activity gives children an opportunity to make observations that relate to several important geometric and measurement ideas. The first observation is that although all the fields are made from the same four Tangram pieces, the fields do not all need the same "lengths" of fencing.

The second observation that children can make is that there are many possible methods of measuring. Using string, or other flexible measuring tools, to find the distance around a shape allows children to measure distance in a non-standard way.

The following chart should resemble the class postings:

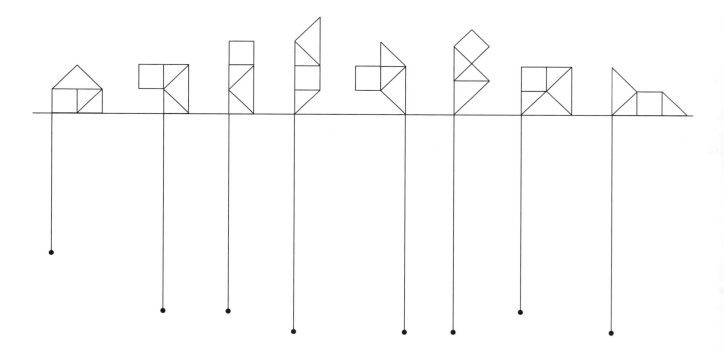

2. Provide children with materials to make three-dimensional models of their fields and fences. Direct them to make clay models of the Tangram pieces they used to make their fields. Have them insert ice cream sticks, or other small sticks, as fenceposts, later gluing a length of string around the sticks.

As children work, they may suggest other ways of measuring the distance around their fields. Using a short side of the small Tangram triangle is one possibility. Children may find it easier using paper clips, rulers, pipe cleaners, straws, or other classroom objects to measure around the fields. Encourage experimentation with different materials.

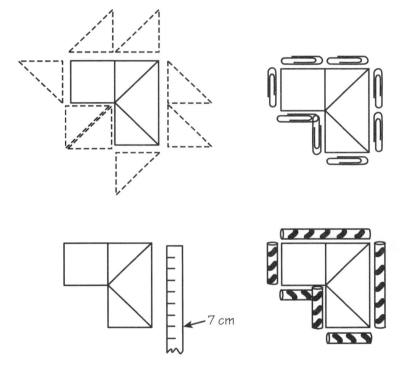

←7 cm

As children come together to share their findings, they may be surprised at how many different fields can be made from the same Tangram pieces. They may also be surprised to find that the distances around the fields vary. Children may have expected that shapes made from the same pieces should have the same perimeter.

As they study the chart—the posted fields and the attached strings representing the fence lengths—children can see how the perimeters vary. Thus, this activity may lead children to gain an understanding of the relationships between area and perimeter.

FLYING FLAGS

- Symmetry
- Spatial visualization
- Transformational geometry

Getting Ready

What You'll Need

Tangrams, 2 sets of 2 different colors per pair

Tangram paper, page 100

Crayons or markers (red, yellow, blue, and green)

Overhead Tangram pieces and/or Tangram paper transparency (optional)

Overview

Children trace Tangram pieces along a vertical line, flip them, and trace them again to make a symmetrical match. In this activity, children have the opportunity to:

- identify and copy geometric shapes
- build an understanding of symmetry
- explore ways in which the position of a shape can be changed

The Activity

You may want to have a child hold the eraser as you trace it each time to suggest how partners should work cooperatively to trace Tangram pieces in On Their Own.

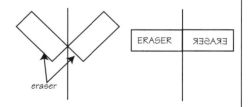

Introducing

- Draw a vertical line on the chalkboard. Hold a chalkboard eraser against the board so that one corner touches the line. Trace around the eraser on the board.
- Still holding the eraser in its original position, demonstrate how to flip the eraser across the line. Trace around it in its new position.
- Ask children what they notice about the two traced shapes. Then reposition the eraser so that at least part of it touches the line and repeat the process.
- Elicit that the two shapes together show *symmetry* because the part of the design on one side of the line is a *mirrored image* of the part on the other side of the line.

On Their Own

How can you fly a Tangram flag?

- With a partner, choose 2 or more Tangram pieces of the same color. You will need these pieces to make a flag.

- Fold a piece of paper in half. Draw a line along the fold. Think of the line as a flagpole.

- Make a 2-piece Tangram flag. Hang your flag from 1 side of the flagpole.

- Pretend it's a windy day! The wind has blown your flag over to the other side of the pole. Use the same Tangram pieces of another color to show how the flag looks now.

- Leave your work so that your classmates can see it.

The Bigger Picture

Thinking and Sharing

Allow pairs to walk around the room to observe one another's flags. Encourage them to compare the flags, looking to see that the flag on one side of a flagpole is the mirrored image of the flag on the other side.

Use prompts such as these to promote class discussion:

- Which side of the flagpole shows how your flag looked before the wind started blowing? Which side shows how it looked after it was blown to the other side of the flagpole?

- Did any flags look exactly like yours? Which ones?

- Were any flags that looked like yours made from different colors? Which colors were they?

- After the wind blew, was it easier to show how one part of your flag looked than another? Why was that part easier to show?

- Why do you think some pieces are easier to show as mirrored images than other pieces?

Drawing

Distribute Tangram paper with a heavy rule drawn on the horizontal line across the middle. Tell children to turn the paper holding it the wide way (so that the heavy rule is vertical). Tell them to pretend that this rule is a flagpole. Have children use one color crayon to trace around and color a flag made from just one Tangram shape. Have them use another color to show how that flag would look after it was blown to the opposite side of the flagpole.

Extending the Activity

Invite children to repeat the activity, this time making three different flags using only the medium triangle. Challenge them to turn the triangle three different ways to make their flags.

Teacher Talk

Where's the Mathematics?

As children try to flip Tangram pieces to show mirrored images, they begin to gain some understanding of geometric properties. They may notice attributes of Tangram pieces such as angles, number and length of sides, and size. They may begin to develop language related to symmetry and other geometric concepts.

Some children may be undecided about which side of the flagpole to hang their flag on. Assure such children that it does not matter which side they choose. They must, however, understand that, after "the wind blows," their flag must look as if it were blown in the exact opposite direction from where it was first hanging. You may want to restate that a flag and its *mirrored image* should each be made from two Tangram pieces that are exactly the same except for color. Some of children's flags, along with their mirrored images, might look like these:

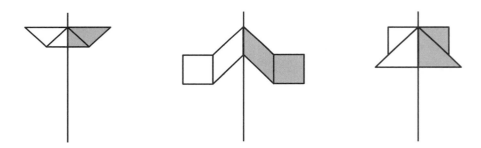

On first glance, some children might fail to recognize that flags exactly like theirs, except for color, have anything in common with theirs. When children begin looking for flags that are like their own, they will probably radiate first towards flags made with the same colors they used. Then, from the group of flags of matching colors, they will look for those with matching shapes.

Children may wish to experiment with mirrored images by flipping a Tangram piece on a point instead of aligning one side with the flagpole. They may notice that when only one point touches the line, it can be difficult to match the angle of the piece to the flagpole.

This can be made clear by modeling the following:

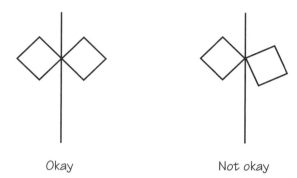

Okay   Not okay

Some children may observe if a mirrored piece is both flipped and rotated, there is no longer a symmetrical match to the original. They may note that the pieces are still the same, but just in new positions. Other children may believe that the two pieces, once turned in this way, no longer form the same shape.

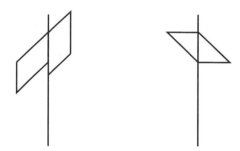

Children may be surprised to realize that a single piece can be used to make different flags. By experimenting with the medium triangle, they may notice that two sides of the triangle are of equal length and one side is longer than the other. Children may incorporate geometric terms into their explanations as they talk about how the placement of this triangle changes from flag to flag.

You may want to encourage children to experiment with different methods for making the flagpole. Some children may notice that they can fold a paper or draw a line at many different angles with respect to the sides of the paper and still place their Tangram flags symmetrically. This exploration may help children discover the importance of the line of symmetry in any symmetrical pattern.

HALF-TIME SHOW

- Spatial reasoning
- Fractions
- Congruence

Getting Ready

What You'll Need

Tangrams, 2 sets of 2 different colors per pair

Small Tangram Triangles, page 101, 10 triangles per pair

Overview

Children use two different colors of Tangram pieces to make a shape in which each colored section covers one half of the shape. In this activity, children have the opportunity to:

- ◆ explore the meaning of one half
- ◆ use small triangles as a unit of measure
- ◆ see that the two halves of a whole have equal areas

The Activity

You may want to encourage children to fold their shapes in order to determine whether or not the parts are halves.

Demonstrate how to use small Tangram triangles to cover shapes. Children can cover the shapes they make in On Their Own *with small triangles. Then they can count them to measure halves.*

Introducing

- ◆ Display these shapes made from red and blue Tangram pieces.
- ◆ Have children copy the shapes, then record them and cut them out.

Shape 1   Shape 2

- ◆ Ask which shape children think has the same amount of red as blue. Have them explain their answers.
- ◆ Point out that Shape 1 is half red and half blue. Elicit that this means that the shape has the same amount of both colors. This is because the two pieces of different colors that make up the shape match exactly.
- ◆ Explain that Shape 2 does not have the same amount of both colors because when the pieces are matched, there is more of one color than the other.

On Their Own

How can you make a Tangram shape that is half 1 color and half another color?

- Work with a partner. Use these Tangram pieces of 1 color. Make any shape you like.

- Now exchange some pieces with those in a Tangram set of another color so that half your shape is the other color.

- Record your shape. Show which pieces are each color.

- Cut out your shape.

- Make other shapes that are half one color and half another color.

- Be ready to talk about how you made your shapes.

The Bigger Picture

Thinking and Sharing

Ask a pair of children to show their shape. Have them post their shape. Then measure each half for them with small Tangram triangles. Write the numbers near the halves. Repeat with other pairs until all shapes are displayed.

Use prompts like these to promote class discussion:

- ◆ What is the same about the posted shapes? What is different?
- ◆ Which posted shapes show halves in the same way? Which show halves in a different way?
- ◆ How can you be sure a shape has the same amount of each color?
- ◆ Are both of these shapes half of one color and half of another? How can you be sure?

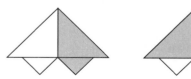

If children discover their shape does not have one half of each color, ask what they would change about the shape. When they have made changes so that they have one half of each color, then add the shape to the board.

Writing

Ask children to tell why it would or would not be possible to share half of a Tangram set with a friend.

Extending the Activity

Have one child make a shape from any four Tangram pieces of a single color. Ask another child to find Tangram pieces of another color and add them to the first shape to make it half one color and half the other color.

Teacher Talk

Where's the Mathematics?

This activity gives children the opportunity to refine their understanding of the meaning of "one half." As they begin the activity, children may use the term "one half" inaccurately. For example, when a shape has more red pieces than blue pieces, they may say "the red half is bigger." With experience, they may discover that for an object to be divided into halves, the two halves must be equal. In this activity, "being equal" means covering the same amount of space or having equal areas. Thus, for one colored section of a shape to be one half of that shape it must cover the same space, or area, as the other section.

Children find measuring colored sections with small Tangram triangles helpful since it gives them a number value to work with. For example, if the complete shape can be covered with 10 small triangles, one half of the shape can be covered with 5 small triangles. Children find that if each colored section of a shape is covered by the same number of small Tangram triangles, then each color covers one half of the shape.

As they build shapes, some children may think that a color does not represent one half if pieces of the same color are not touching as shown below.

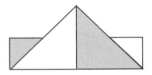

Other children may think that only symmetrical shapes with the second color mirroring the first color can show halves.

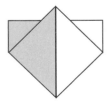

Children should then work together using small triangles to measure the amount of each color to prove that each represents one half of the whole shape.

As children gain experience using small triangles to measure shapes, they begin to discover that the placement of the color does not affect the shape's total area.

Some examples of children's work are shown below.

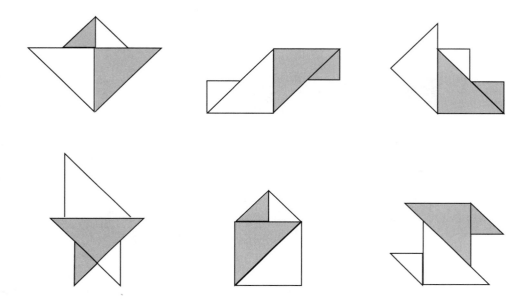

As children check their work, some may be satisfied that a color represents one half as long as the same pieces of both colors are used in the shape. Other children may rely on measuring the area with small triangles to confirm their work. Either way, the activity gives children the chance to visualize one half and helps them to understand that halves of a whole can have different shapes.

MAKING A QUILT

- Spatial visualization
- Looking for patterns
- Transformational geometry
- Congruence

Getting Ready

What You'll Need

Tangrams, 2 sets of 2 different colors per pair

Nine-Patch Quilt outline, 1 per group, page 92

Crayons or markers (red, yellow, blue, green)

Construction paper (6-in.-square piece), 1 per group

Paste

Overhead Tangram pieces and/or *Nine-Patch Quilt* transparency (optional)

Overview

Children make paper quilts based on quilt-square patterns they design using Tangram triangles. In this activity, children have the opportunity to:

◆ explore relationships among Tangram pieces

◆ arrange Tangram pieces to form a design

◆ repeat a design to form a pattern

The Activity

You may want to familiarize children with the history of patchwork quilt-making and with some of the many possible quilt patterns by reading aloud from any of the following books: A Cloak for the Dreamer, Eight Hands Round: A Patchwork Alphabet, The Keeping Quilt, The Josefina Story Quilt, Texas Star, *and* The Patchwork Quilt.

Introducing

◆ Hold up two Tangram parallelograms of different colors. Explain that these pieces can be used together to make different designs.

◆ Invite volunteers to model the ways in which the parallelograms can be put together with complete sides touching to form designs.

◆ Call for a show of hands, allowing children to vote on the design they like best.

◆ Record the preferred design in color in the middle of a piece of Tangram paper.

◆ Now, challenge children to suggest how you could make a pattern by repeating the design on the paper using crayons alone.

◆ Follow children's directions, then display the pattern.

On Their Own

How can you use Tangram pieces to make a quilt pattern?

- Work in a group. Take these Tangram pieces from 2 sets of different colors.

1 medium triangle
2 small triangles   1 medium triangle
2 small triangles

- Use any 3 of the pieces to make a square design.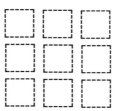

- Record your design in each of the squares on a piece of Nine-Patch Quilt paper that looks like this:

- Cut out each square.

- Arrange the squares in 3 rows and 3 columns. You may exchange 1 square for another until you find the pattern you like best.

- Paste your pattern on construction paper to make a quilt.

- Be ready to talk about how you made your design and your quilt.

The Bigger Picture

Thinking and Sharing

Have children post their quilts. You may wish to have quilts of like colors grouped together to make it easy to compare them.

Use prompts such as these to promote class discussion:

- How did you decide which Tangram pieces to use for your design?

- What words can you use to describe your design?

- How did you decide on your pattern when you were putting the nine squares together?

- How could different patterns be made from your design?

- Are any of the posted patterns exactly like yours? Which ones?

- Would any patterns that are different from yours become exactly the same if some of the designs were turned? if some of the pieces in the design were flipped? Explain.

Extending the Activity

Have groups begin the activity again. This time, have them fill two *Nine-Patch Quilt* outlines. Direct children to record and color their design on one of the outlines to match the Tangram pieces they used. On the other outline, have them record their design using a different color scheme. Distribute

Teacher Talk

Where's the Mathematics?

As children repeat a pattern to form quilt patterns, they have many opportunities to use the language of geometry. Children may be surprised that the simple square design, when repeated, can make a visually exciting pattern.

With three pieces in two colors to choose from, children can make six unique square designs. You may want to point out how each design looks after 1/4, 1/2, and 3/4 turns. The designs below have been turned to the left.

Most children will have no problem fitting their Tangram pieces together to form a square. If they do have trouble, have them start by positioning the medium triangle so that the square corner of the triangle matches one of the square corners of a quilt-square outline.

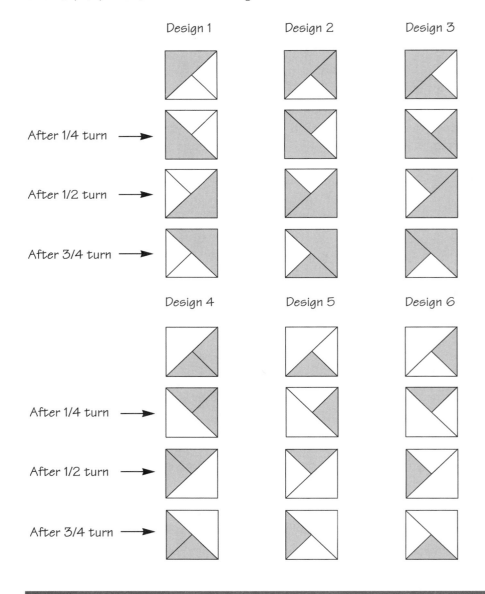

6-by-12-inch pieces of construction paper, each folded into eighteen squares. Tell the groups to cut out and combine their pieces to make a pattern of squares in six rows and three columns. Have them then paste their pattern on the construction paper to form a double-size quilt.

As children record Tangram pieces to make their square designs, they may observe that a quilt square can be divided into two medium Tangram triangles and that two small Tangram triangles cover the same space, or have the same area, as the medium Tangram triangle.

In pasting their designs to make a quilt, some children may have difficulty turning the squares to make a consistent pattern. Children who are able to identify their pattern in some way may have an easier time repeating it. For example, some children may say that they see their pattern as forming mountains, a road, or the letters K or V.

As children discuss the completed quilts, some may notice that small shapes in the square design can become parts of the pattern in the quilt. Children with a good sense of spatial visualization may see that changes in the color and direction of the original design may result in dramatic changes in the overall appearance of the quilt.

One group's quilt may look like this.

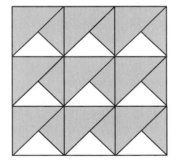

Notice how the pattern above would look if some of the squares undergo a 1/4 turn, then if some of the pieces in the original design are flipped.

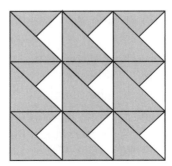
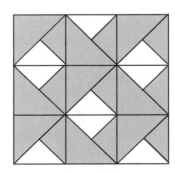

MIRROR MAGICIAN

- **Symmetry**
- **Spatial visualization**
- **Transformational geometry**

Getting Ready

What You'll Need

Tangrams, 2 sets of 1 color per pair

Paper, 1 sheet per pair

Mirror, 1 per pair (optional)

Overhead Tangram pieces and/or Tangram paper transparency (optional)

Overview

In this game for two players, children build mirrored images of Tangram shapes in an effort to form patterns that have line symmetry. In this activity, children have the opportunity to:

- ◆ develop a recognition of symmetry
- ◆ practice left-right differentiation
- ◆ think about how to describe a shape's location with respect to the location of its reflected image

← A mirror line

The Activity

Reinforce the idea that each child's stance is a mirrored image of the other's. You may do this by pointing out, for example, that while one child's right hand is on his hip, the other child's left hand is on her hip.

As an alternative to this introduction you may wish to have children demonstrate symmetry at the chalkboard as shown above.

Introducing

- ◆ Draw a chalk line about three feet long on the floor. Tell children to pretend that the line is an invisible mirror.

- ◆ Call on a child to stand on one side of the line and to take a particular stance, such as with one hand on a hip and the other hand covering an ear.

- ◆ Invite another child to be a "Mirror Magician." Explain that the Mirror Magician's job is to stand on the other side of the line, to pretend to be facing a mirror, and to do what the other child is doing as if he or she were seeing it in the mirror.

- ◆ Have the class talk about how the Mirror Magician is reflecting the first child's stance. If it is not being done correctly, call for suggestions how on the Mirror Magician can correct the stance.

- ◆ Call on another child to decide on a new stance to take on one side of the line. Have another Mirror Magician show the stance that would be reflected in mirror on the other side of the line, explaining what he or she is doing.

On Their Own

Play *Mirror Magician!*

Here are the rules.

1. This is a game for 2 players. The object is to show the mirrored images of 4 Tangram pieces. Players decide who will be the Chooser and who will be the Mirror Magician.

2. Players fold a piece of paper in half. They pretend that the fold line is a mirror.

3. The Chooser picks a Tangram piece and places it on the paper. One side of the piece must be against the line, touching the "mirror."

4. The Mirror Magician places a matching piece on the other side of the line to show how the piece would look in a mirror.

5. Now, the Chooser puts down 3 more pieces. The Mirror Magician finds and puts down the mirrored image of each one.

6. Players record the pieces and their mirrored images.

- Play 4 games of Mirror Magician. Take turns being the Chooser and the Mirror Magician.

- Be ready to tell how you decided where to put your pieces when you were the Mirror Magician.

The Bigger Picture

Thinking and Sharing

Invite children to talk about their games and describe some of the thinking they did. Ask children to post some of their recordings on the board.

Use prompts such as these to promote class discussion:

- What do you notice about all of the recordings?

- How can you be sure that what you see on one side of the fold is a mirrored image of what is on the other side?

- When it was your turn to be the Mirror Magician, how did you decide where to put your piece?

- When you were the Mirror Magician, which pieces were the easiest to put down? Which were the hardest?

- Would the pieces in your recording still look like mirrored images of each other if you turned your paper upside down? Explain.

Drawing and Writing

Have children fold a piece of paper in half, then open the paper to lie flat. Show them how to put a few drops of paint on one half of the paper. Have them press down the other half of the paper to spread the paint. After they carefully pull apart the two halves, ask children to tell how the picture they are looking at is like their *Mirror Magician* recordings.

Teacher Talk

Where's the Mathematics?

As children use Tangram pieces to make mirrored images, they begin to recognize line symmetry. Some may be able to sight symmetry, but not be able to describe how they know that one side mirrors the other. Others may talk about one side being the *opposite* or a *backwards match* of what is on the other side of the line.

While in the role of Mirror Magician, children may develop various strategies for making the mirrored images. Some may choose to hold a Tangram piece in the same orientation as the original and then flip it over. This method helps children see the relationship between the original shape and its mirrored image.

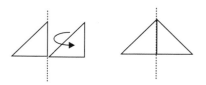

As children work, they may be surprised to find out that there is only one position in which a matching piece can be placed to make the mirrored image. Children may find it helpful to record each piece after it is placed so that they can fold the paper to check its placement. Children could also use small mirrors as they work to see how the mirrored images should look when reflected in a mirror. If they do this, be sure they understand how to position the mirror on the line of symmetry so that it reflects the original piece. Then, what they see in the mirror shows the orientation of the mirrored image.

Some common errors children may make in trying to show the mirrored image are (A) not flipping a piece, (B) positioning a piece too far from the fold line, and (C) positioning a mirrored piece above or below the original piece.

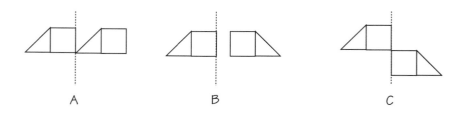

A   B   C

Extending the Activity

Have children repeat the activity, this time using a piece of paper that has been folded diagonally.

Most children will have little trouble deciding how to put down the mirrored image of the square Tangram piece because the piece itself is symmetrical. Children will probably find that the parallelogram is the hardest piece to put down. Orienting the mirrored images of all three sizes of triangles will pose a challenge to many children as well.

Some samples of children's *Mirror Magician* recordings are shown below:

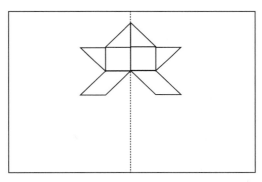
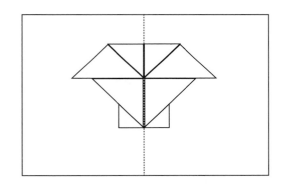
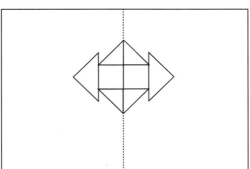
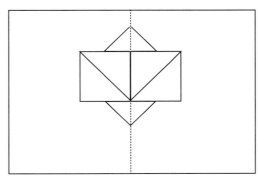

RECTANGLE RACE

- Chance
- Counting
- Comparing
- Congruence
- Spatial visualization
- Game strategies

Getting Ready

What You'll Need

Tangrams, 2 sets of 2 different colors per pair

Number cube (marked 1-6) or die, 1 per pair

Rectangle Race game board, 1 per pair, page 93

Overhead Tangram pieces and/or *Rectangle Race* game board transparency (optional)

Overview

In this game for two players, children take turns placing Tangram pieces on a game board according to a roll of a number cube in an effort to be the one to put down the last piece. In this activity, children have the opportunity to:

- ◆ find the number of Tangram pieces that match the roll of a number cube
- ◆ observe the way Tangram pieces can be combined into a rectangular configuration
- ◆ discover playing strategies

The Activity

*Prepare, or have children prepare,
Rectangle Race game boards by first
cutting to separate the two parts of the
game board, then cutting along the
dotted end of each part and taping the
pieces together at these ends.*

Introducing

- ◆ Prepare, then display, this square outline made from four Tangram pieces.
- ◆ Call on a volunteer to match one Tangram piece to one part of the outline and to cover that part with the piece.
- ◆ Invite three more volunteers to match pieces until the complete outline is covered.
- ◆ Together with the children, count the number of pieces needed to cover the square outline. Be sure that children understand that four pieces were needed to cover it completely.

On Their Own

Play *Rectangle Race!*

Here are the rules.

1. This is a game for 2 players. The object is to place the last Tangram piece on the game board.

2. Each player uses 1 color of Tangram pieces. Players choose colors and decide who will go first.

3. Players take turns rolling a number cube and placing that number of their Tangram pieces on a game board that looks like this:

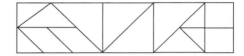

4. The winner is the one who places the last piece on the game board. You don't need to roll the exact number to place the last piece.

- Play *Rectangle Race* 4 times. Take turns going first.
- Be ready to talk about good moves and bad moves.

The Bigger Picture

Thinking and Sharing

Invite children to talk about their games and describe some of the thinking they did.

Use prompts such as these to promote class discussion:

- On your turn, did it matter which Tangram pieces you placed on the board? Explain.
- Did the order in which you placed your pieces matter? Explain.
- Is it possible to win this game after just one roll? after just two rolls?
- When would it be good to roll a high number? a low number?
- Do you think both players have a fair chance of winning this game?

Writing

Ask children to write, or record on an audio cassette, a letter to a friend in which they describe this game and give advice about how to be good at playing it.

Extending the Activity

1. Have children play *Rectangle Race* again, this time counting the number of pieces they each placed on the board. The winner is the player who placed the greater number of pieces.

Teacher Talk

Where's the Mathematics?

As children decide which Tangram pieces to place on the game board, they are exploring game strategies. The first few times children play the game, they may believe that the best moves result from rolling the higher number or from placing the biggest pieces first. As they gain experience, they may notice that it is the number of pieces, not the size of the pieces, that affects the outcome of the game. This can be made clear by showing the board below, which reflects each player's first turn. Each rolled a 4. One player put down large triangles, thus covering more of the board than the other player did. Point out, however, that the size of the pieces does not matter. What is important is that 6 empty spaces remain.

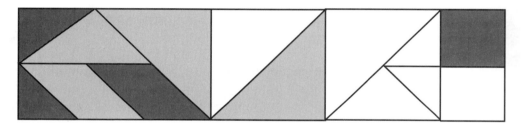

After a few games, children may notice how what happens in one turn affects what might happen in a later turn. Children may begin to count how many empty spaces are left to figure out whether they want to roll a high or low number. You may want to point out that on each turn there is an equally likely chance of rolling any of the numbers from 1 to 6. Sometimes, however, even those children who understand this continue to wish for a roll of a particular number. In the game shown below, for example, the first player rolled a 5, leaving 9 empty spaces. The second player may realize that rolling a low number on her turn will make it harder, or impossible, for the first player to win on his next turn.

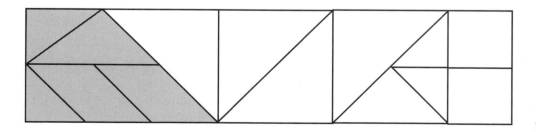

2. Have children play the game as before, but this time require that players roll the exact number of empty spaces to place the final piece.

By taking turns going first, children gather data about whether the game is fair. Some children may believe the player who goes first will always win. As they gather evidence to the contrary, some may decide that both players have a fair chance of winning. Others may hold onto the idea that "first is best" or they may decide that the second player will always win. You may want to have children keep track of what happened in each of their games in a chart like this one:

Children may talk about being lucky *or* unlucky *as they play the game. If you hear this kind of discussion, model correct mathematical language including the use of the words* always, never, likely, unlikely, possible, *and* probably.

Game	Who Went First?	Who Won the Game?
1	David	Maggie
2	Maggie	David
3	David	Maggie
4	Maggie	Maggie

Be sure that children have played the game at least four times before they begin to speculate about fairness. Some children may decide the game must not be fair if one player wins twice in a row. These children associate "fairness" with what happens, not with what could happen. As children listen to the experiences of other pairs, they may conclude that either player could win two games each, although that may not have happened as they played.

Children may suggest many possible strategies for playing to win. Some children may suggest that keeping track of how many pieces are left is a good way to know what number you want to roll. Others may observe that there is no way to control what number you will roll so there is no way to be sure of winning the game.

SAILING ALONG

Getting Ready

What You'll Need

Tangrams, 4 sets per group

Sailboat outline, 1 per pair, page 94

Large Tangram Triangle outlines, page 95

Overhead Tangram set and/or Sailboat outline transparency (optional)

Overview

Children use Tangram pieces to fill in the outline of a sailboat, first using the least number, then the greatest number, of pieces possible. In this activity, children have the opportunity to:

◆ develop strategies for filling an outline with Tangram pieces

◆ discover that certain combinations of Tangram pieces can be exchanged for other pieces

The Activity

Introducing

◆ Distribute the outline of large Tangram triangles, (see page 95).

◆ Ask a child to show how to fill one of the triangles using just one Tangram piece.

◆ Invite a volunteer to fill another triangle using exactly two pieces.

◆ Have other volunteers fill a triangle using exactly three pieces, then exactly four pieces. Invite children to show other possible arrangements of three pieces and four pieces.

◆ Ask children if they think it is possible to fill the large triangle with more than four pieces. Have them explain their reasoning.

On Their Own

What is the least number of Tangram pieces that will fill the sailboat outline? What is the greatest number of pieces that will fill it?

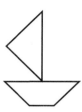

- Work in a group. Use Tangram pieces to exactly fill a sailboat outline like this one:

- Count how many pieces you used.

- Look for a way to use fewer pieces to fill the outline.
  Try again until you have used the least number of pieces you can.
  Then write down that number.

- Now look for a way to use more pieces. Try again until you have used the greatest number of pieces you can. Write down that number.

- Be ready to talk about the ways you filled your outline.

The Bigger Picture

Thinking and Sharing

Make a two-column list on the board and label the columns *Least* and *Greatest*. Ask groups to tell the least and greatest numbers of pieces they used to fill the sailboat outline. List the numbers in the correct columns on the board. When the list is finished, ask children why some of the numbers are the same. Have children determine the least and greatest of all the numbers in each column.

Use prompts like these to promote class discussion:

- ◆ What do you notice about all the different ways you filled the sailboat outline?

- ◆ What did you do to fill in the outline with the least number of pieces?

- ◆ What did you do to fill in the outline with the greatest number of pieces?

- ◆ How did you know that you had found the least number of pieces? the greatest number of pieces?

- ◆ What can you do to cover any Tangram shape with the greatest number of pieces?

Extending the Activity

Have children work in pairs to design a pine tree shape using Tangram pieces. Allow them to tape the pieces together and trace them to create an outline. Have them exchange outlines with another pair, then try to fill each other's outlines with the least and greatest numbers of Tangram pieces possible.

You may want to prepare this outline using a square and one each of the large, medium, and small triangles.

Where's the Mathematics?

As children work to fill in the sailboat outline with the least and greatest number of pieces, they practice both counting and interchanging geometric shapes. As they experiment, they begin to understand how Tangram shapes are related.

When covering the sail (the large triangle) with smaller pieces, children have the opportunity to see that small Tangram shapes can be combined to make larger shapes. The following combinations are possible:

Different Ways to Cover the Sail

1 Tangram piece

2 Tangram pieces

3 Tangram pieces

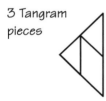

4 Tangram pieces

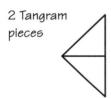 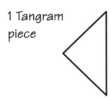

In finding the least number of pieces needed to fill the sailboat outline, children may first take the largest Tangram pieces to see how they fit. Working in small groups and observing others, some children may see which pieces can reasonably fit into the outline and which cannot.

Children may start with small pieces and substitute larger ones for them in order to use fewer pieces. For example, they may substitute a parallelogram, a square, or a medium triangle for two small triangles.

Some children may also work in steps to find the greatest number of pieces needed to build the sailboat. For example, when filling the sailboat's sail, some children may first replace the large triangle with the next largest pieces, the two medium triangles. Others may start with small triangles because they have already noticed that, by using small triangles, they can cover any Tangram shape with the greatest number of pieces possible. When covering shapes with small triangles, children may begin to understand the significance of unit measurement or how a unit is used to measure the area of a shape.

Children may discuss the different strategies they used to exchange Tangram pieces as they found their sailboat solutions.

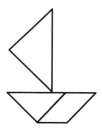

Least Number
of Pieces (3)

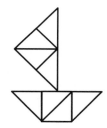

Greatest Number
of Pieces (8)

As children explore different ways to fill the outline, they may observe that the least number of pieces possible depends on the particular arrangement of the medium triangle and the parallelogram, whereas the greatest number depends on the arrangement of small triangles.

SAME AND DIFFERENT

- Comparing
- Counting
- Spatial visualization

Getting Ready

What You'll Need

Tangrams, 1 set per child

Overhead Tangram pieces and/or Tangram paper transparency (optional)

Overview

Children make shapes from four Tangram pieces of their own choosing. Then they compare their shapes, discussing how they are alike and how they are different. In this activity, children have the opportunity to:

- ◆ recognize that shapes can be described in relation to other shapes
- ◆ understand the meanings of *same* and *different*
- ◆ develop and use language related to geometric concepts

The Activity

Try, when possible, to elicit what makes the pieces different, not by saying, for example "One is a square, the other is not," but by saying, "One is a square, the other is a triangle."

If children are having difficulty, ask them questions about specific attributes such as number of sides, length of sides, number of corners, angles, color, number of pieces, kind of pieces, symmetry (within each piece), size, and position.

Introducing

- ◆ Remove the parallelogram and a small triangle from a Tangram set and display them.
- ◆ Have children talk to their partners about the ways in which the pieces are the same. Then call on volunteers to share their discussions.
- ◆ Now ask children to talk with their partners about how the two pieces are different. Have volunteers share their ideas.
- ◆ Repeat this process for other pairs of pieces until you feel that children are ready for *On Their Own*.

On Their Own

How can a Tangram shape that you make be the same as your partner's? How can these shapes be different?

- Work with a partner.

- Choose 4 pieces from your Tangram set. Use the pieces to make a shape. Put your shape next to your partner's shape.

- Look at both shapes carefully. Then talk to your partner about the ways your shapes are the same. Give all the ideas you can.

- Talk about the ways your shapes are different.

- Record your shapes.

- Be ready to tell other children what you found out about your 2 shapes.

The Bigger Picture

Thinking and Sharing

Invite a pair to display their shapes. Then ask them to tell how their shapes are the same and how they are different. Record their responses in a two-column chart under the headings *Same* and *Different*. Allow other pairs to share their shapes. Lead a class discussion about each pair of shapes and chart their similarities and differences.

Use prompts such as these to promote class discussion:

- What did you notice first about your shape and your partner's?

- How could you describe one of the posted shapes to someone else?

- Are shapes made from the same number of pieces always the same size? Explain.

- What is the same about *all* the posted shapes? Are they all different in any way? Explain.

Writing

Have children write down a list of things that can be compared in their Tangram shapes, for example, size.

Extending the Activity

Have children repeat the activity, this time allowing them to make shapes using four pieces taken from two Tangram sets of different colors.

Where's the Mathematics?

In addition to counting and comparing Tangram pieces used to form shapes, this activity gives children the chance to compare the properties of both individual pieces and combined shapes. It leads children to begin to think about how objects may be compared according to number, color, size, and shape.

Children may find there are many things to look at when comparing two shapes, such as the number of pieces and the size of pieces they contain. As partners explore similarities and differences between their shapes, they will probably first notice which pieces their shapes have in common. Then they will focus on likenesses and/or differences in color and in the relative positions of the pieces that make up the shapes.

As children create and compare new shapes, they may notice that larger shapes are not always made from more Tangram pieces than are smaller shapes. When two shapes have been made from the same Tangram pieces, children may notice how different the shapes look, how much shorter, wider, longer, or thinner one is than the other.

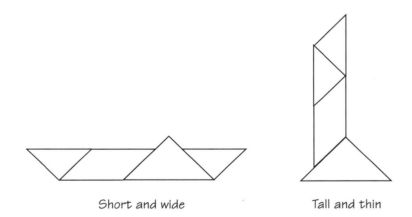

Short and wide   Tall and thin

As they work, some children may see that some Tangram pieces can be made from others. For example, they may notice that two small triangles can be put together to make a square. These concepts build a foundation for understanding units of measurement and measuring the area of a shape. For children's use in recording their work you may want to give them a list of attribute words, such as, *large, small, corners, sides, color,* and *shapes.* Children may also draw pictures to show their ideas.

Some samples of partners' recordings of their two shapes are shown below.

Each shape has 5 sides.
The shapes are the same but have some different pieces.

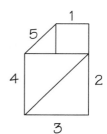 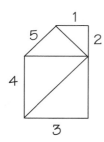

Each shape has 2 colors.
Each shape has a square piece.

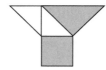 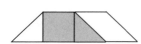

One shape is small. One is large.
The shapes point in different directions.

 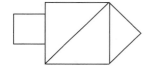

When two colors are used to make a shape, children may make observations about symmetry or asymmetry. They may also make observations about which fractional parts of the whole shape different colors represent.

When a shape is made from two colors, young children may believe each color always represents one half, whether or not the same amount of the shape is covered by each color.

Both sides of the shape are
the same. Each color covers
1/2 of the shape.

SECRET BUILDER

- Spatial visualization
- Properties of geometric shapes
- Following directions

Getting Ready

What You'll Need

Tangrams, 1 set per child

Tangram paper, page 100

Overhead Tangram pieces and/or Tangram paper transparency (optional)

Overview

Children take turns making secret shapes from Tangram pieces. They describe their shapes to their partners, who try to make the shapes from the directions they are given. In this activity, children have the opportunity to:

- identify attributes of Tangram shapes
- communicate specific information
- develop listening and problem-solving skills

The Activity

You may want to have children copy the clues in order to share the activity with family members at home.

Introducing

- Show children this Tangram shape: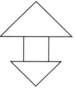
- Ask volunteers to give clues about the shape so that someone who could not see it would know what it looks like. Write each of their clues on the chalkboard.
- Discuss which clues best tell about the shape and which might be confusing and why.
- Try to get a consensus about which clues work together best to describe the shape.

On Their Own

Can you tell someone how to make a secret Tangram shape?

- Work with a partner. Decide who will be the first Secret Builder.
- The Secret Builder:
  - Secretly chooses 3 or more Tangram pieces.
  - Makes a secret shape from the 3 pieces.
  - Gives clues about the shape to help the partner make the shape.
- The partner listens carefully and tries to make the shape.
- When the partner is ready, the Secret Builder shows his or her shape. Partners check to see if the two shapes match.
- Do this 3 more times. Take turns being the Secret Builder.
- Be ready to talk about making secret shapes and giving clues about them.

The Bigger Picture

Thinking and Sharing

Ask a pair to display the last two shapes they made. Have the Secret Builder try to recall the clues he or she gave. Then invite the class to comment on the clues and on the shapes. Repeat this process with a few other pairs.

Use prompts such as these to promote class discussion:

- Were some clues more helpful than others? Explain.
- What words did you use to describe the different Tangram pieces?
- What words helped you know how to put down pieces or line them up?
- Which pieces were the easiest to explain? the hardest?
- Did it help if the Secret Builder first told you which pieces were in the shape? Why?
- Which shapes were the easiest to make? the hardest?

You may want to suggest that children place pieces so that the sides touch. Explain that it is hard to know how to follow clues about a shape when only one point of a piece is touching another.

easy to follow clues

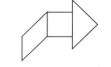

hard to follow clues

Drawing and Writing

Have children draw several three-piece secret shapes on sheets of Tangram paper. Suggest that they look carefully at their shapes to find one that reminds them of a familiar object. When they have found one, have them circle it. Then, on the back of the paper, have them write clues about the chosen shape, one of which may name the familiar object. Tell children to exchange papers and to try to follow each other's clues to make the shapes.

Extending the Activity

1. Have partners play the game again. This time, the Secret Builder can answer questions to describe the shape. For example, a partner may ask the Secret Builder, "Which pieces are in the shape?" or "Should I put the square above the small triangle?"

Where's the Mathematics?

As children give clues for building shapes and respond to these clues, they gain experience in using and interpreting mathematical language.

As they describe their shapes, some children may use geometric names for the Tangram pieces (*triangle*, *parallelogram*, and *square*). Others may choose to use descriptive words for the pieces. For example, the parallelogram might be called the "leaning" piece.

Children will develop different strategies for giving clues about their shapes. Some may begin by naming each piece in the shape. Others may start with an overall description. For example, a child might give these clues about the pictured shapes below:

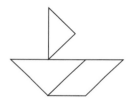

Clues
1. Two of the pieces have square corners.
2. The larger piece with a square corner touches a complete side of the piece that has no square corners.
3. The smaller piece with a square corner touches the middle of the longest side of the larger piece with a square corner.
4. The shape looks like a sailboat.

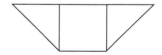

Clues
1. All the pieces have at least one square corner.
2. Two of the pieces are exactly the same.
3. Each piece touches a complete side of another piece.
4. The shape looks like a trapezoid.

2. Have pairs work together to design a shape. Then have them either write a set of clues or record clues on audio tape. Have them exchange clues with another pair of students and try to make the shapes from the clues.

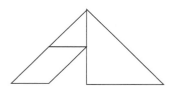

Clues
1. The shape looks like a slide with a ladder.
2. The side of the ladder is made from two pieces.
3. The slide is made from one piece.
4. The top of the ladder touches the top of the slide.

As children gain experience describing shapes, they may realize that people see things differently. What looks like a sailboat to one child may look like a candle to another child. As children take turns being the Secret Builder, they may begin to understand that describing a shape in more than one way improves their partners' chances for success.

As each Secret Builder and partner compare their shapes, some may focus exclusively on whether the partner was right or wrong. Others may talk about which parts of the shape are the same and which parts are different. You may hear comments such as "You almost had it" or "I should have told you to turn the triangle sideways." Such comments reflect children's understanding that the Secret Builder has an equal responsibility in making the shape an exact copy of the original.

As children continue to build shapes and to try to copy them from clues, they may begin to develop shortcuts for describing common formations or may refer to previously made shapes. These experiences help children build a meaningful geometric vocabulary.

SHAPE MORPHER

- Spatial visualization
- Shape recognition
- Deductive reasoning

Getting Ready

What You'll Need

Tangrams, 1 set per child

Overhead Tangram pieces and/or Tangram paper transparency (optional)

Overview

In this game for four or more players, children take turns being the Shape Morpher who creates and changes a shape using four Tangram pieces. The other players try to make matching shapes. In this activity, children have the opportunity to:

- copy and compare shapes
- recognize changes in shapes
- explore the properties of shapes

The Activity

If overhead Tangrams are available, use them to display your shape, then turn off the projector while making the change in the shape and turn it on again to display the new shape.

In the On Their Own activity, children may need to move around and view shapes from different angles in order to copy shapes.

Introducing

- Display this shape. Have children duplicate it with their Tangrams.

- Tell children you are going to move one piece to change the shape. Have children close their eyes or look away. As they do, move the medium triangle to form this shape.

- Ask children to identify the piece you moved. Have children match your shape by making the same move with their Tangram piece.

- Again, have children close their eyes, then move a small triangle to form this shape.

- Challenge children to identify the change and match the new shape with their own pieces.

On Their Own

Play *Shape Morpher!*

Here are the rules:

1. This is a game for 4 to 6 players. The object is to match changes made in a Tangram shape.

2. Players sit in a circle. They decide who will be the Shape Morpher.

3. The Shape Morpher chooses 4 Tangram pieces and uses them all to make a shape.

4. The other players use their Tangram pieces to copy the shape.

5. Players close their eyes. The Shape Morpher secretly moves 1 piece to change the shape.

6. Then players open their eyes. They try to figure out which piece was moved. They make the same change to their shapes.

7. Each of the players takes a turn secretly changing the shape. The others try to match each change.

- Play again until everyone has a chance to be the Shape Morpher.

- Be ready to talk about your moves.

The Bigger Picture

Thinking and Sharing

Invite children to talk about their games and describe some of the thinking they did.

Use prompts like these to promote class discussion:

- How could you tell which piece the Shape Morpher moved?
- Were certain shapes easier or harder to copy than others? Which ones? Why?
- When you were the Shape Morpher, how did you decide which piece to move?
- How could you move a piece to make the shape hard to copy? easy to copy?
- Which did you like better—being the Shape Morpher or being one of the other players? Why?

Drawing and Writing

Ask children to trace a shape made from four Tangram pieces. Then have them move one of the pieces and trace the "morphed" shape. Ask them to compare the shapes.

Extending the Activity

1. Have children play the game again, this time allowing the Shape Morpher to move two pieces at a time.

2. Playing in groups of six to eight, have children play again, this time using all seven Tangram pieces.

Where's the Mathematics?

As children copy changes in shapes, they are simply rearranging the same four pieces. Thus they gain experience in recognizing Tangram pieces in various orientations. Since the pieces cover the same amount of space each time a piece is moved, children gain an intuitive understanding that moving a piece does not change the area of the shape.

As they make and copy shapes, some children may be able to identify some of these shapes by name:

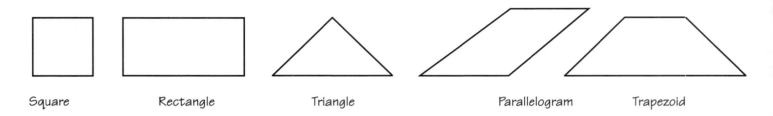

Square   Rectangle   Triangle   Parallelogram   Trapezoid

Children may find it easier to spot a change in these more commonly seen shapes. Since the shape is familiar, they can easily see where a piece was taken from and where it has been moved to.

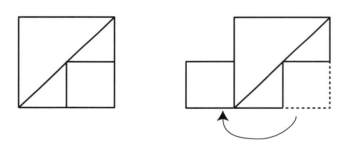

When the shape formed is not as familiar or when the sides and edges of the pieces in a shape do not line up, children may have difficulty identifying which piece was moved.

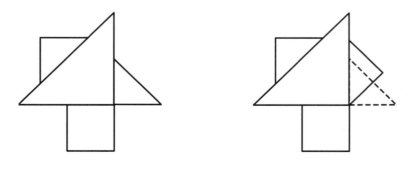

Some children may decide that changes in pieces which "stick out" are easiest to find.

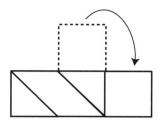

Children may find it more difficult to spot the moving of larger pieces, since these make the greatest amount of change in the shape. Changes made with small pieces are usually easier for children to find.

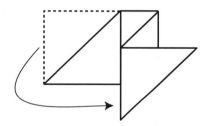

Moving a piece so that one familiar polygon is changed into a completely different one may be the most difficult for children to see because they are focusing on the shape and not on the pieces that make up the shape.

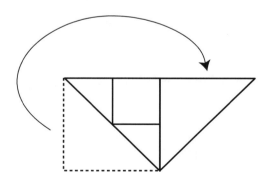

SHAPES WITHIN SHAPES

- Shape fitting
- Counting
- Properties of geometric shapes
- Congruence

Getting Ready

What You'll Need

Tangrams, 2 sets of 1 color per pair

Large Tangram Triangles worksheet, 2 per pair, page 95

Overhead Tangram pieces and/or Tangram paper transparency (optional)

Overview

Children explore different ways to fill an outline of the large Tangram triangle with other Tangram pieces. In this activity, children have the opportunity to:

◆ discover that certain Tangram pieces can be made from combinations of other pieces

◆ count the number of smaller pieces needed to cover a larger piece

The Activity

Introducing

◆ Display a 5-cm-by-10-cm rectangular outline.

◆ Explain that the outline can be filled with Tangram pieces. Place two small triangles and a medium triangle on the outline to show one way to fill it.

◆ Ask children to suggest other ways to fill the outline. Most children will find these two ways.

◆ If no one suggests these additional ways to fill the outline, display them. Call on volunteers to tell how these ways differ from the others.

On Their Own

How many different ways can you use Tangram pieces to fill the outline of the large Tangram triangle?

- With a partner, cover 1 large Tangram triangle exactly using other Tangram pieces.

- Record your work on 1 triangle on a worksheet that looks like this:

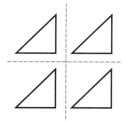

- Count the number of pieces you used. Write that next to the triangle.

- Now find as many different ways as you can to use Tangram pieces to cover a large triangle. Record each way. Count and write the number of pieces that you use for each.

The Bigger Picture

Thinking and Sharing

Invite one pair to post their solutions. Ask other pairs who have different solutions to post them. Continue this process until all eight solutions have been posted.

Use prompts like these to promote class discussion:

- ◆ Which Tangram pieces did you use to cover the large Tangram triangle?

- ◆ What was the least number of pieces you used to fill a triangle outline? What was the greatest number of pieces?

- ◆ What helped you find new ways to fill the triangle outline?

- ◆ Are these two outlines filled the same way? Explain.

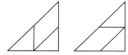

- ◆ How many different ways did you find to fill the triangle? Do you think you found them all? Why?

Writing

Suggest that children choose their outlines that are filled with exactly the same Tangram pieces. Then, have them describe how the outlines are different.

Extending the Activity

Have children put two Tangram pieces together with sides touching to make a shape. Have them trace the shape (first taping the pieces together, if necessary). Then have them fill in the traced outline using other Tangram pieces.

Where's the Mathematics?

With piece and position (and not color) as factors, there are eight different ways to fill the large triangle with smaller pieces:

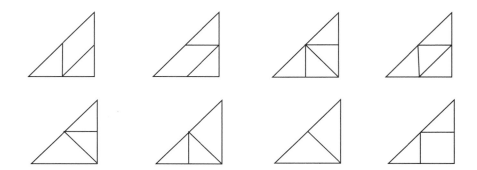

The solutions are all made by fitting two, three, or four Tangram pieces into the outline of the large Tangram triangle.

Children who rely on flipping pieces may believe the following solutions to be different. Other children may insist they are the same.

Children may discover that there are many ways to go about looking for these solutions. After finding one solution, some children may simply move the same pieces around, looking for another. Other children may rotate or flip the entire shapes they have made.

Some children may conclude that the eight solutions shown above are the only possible solutions. Other children may discuss ideas such as substituting some pieces for the same pieces of different colors to make different

Have children record their work. Then challenge children to find any other way to fill the shape and record it.

designs. The number of possible solutions will always depend on how "different" was defined by each pair.

In addition to counting and fitting Tangrams together, this activity gives children the chance to observe that a large shape can be made from smaller shapes. As children experiment with different ways to fill the large triangle outline, they may discover that certain combinations of shapes are interchangeable. For example, the parallelogram, the square, and the medium triangle can each be replaced with two small Tangram triangles.

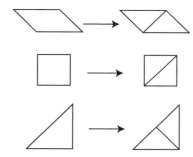

As children explore covering the same shape with smaller pieces, they may observe that even the large Tangram triangle can be covered using all small triangles, and that by using all small triangles they can be certain of using the greatest possible number of pieces. This can be shown in two ways:

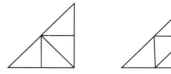

This idea of covering shapes with all small triangles sets a foundation for understanding units of measurement and for measuring the area of shapes with non-standard units of measurement.

TAN DESIGNS

- Sorting
- Counting
- Graphing
- Congruence

Getting Ready

What You'll Need

Tangrams, 3 sets per pair

Tan Designs worksheet, 1 per group, page 96

Overhead Tangram set and/or *Tan Designs* worksheet transparency (optional)

Overview

Children fill a rectangular outline with Tangram pieces, then record the pieces and the number of each kind of piece they used. In this activity, children have the opportunity to:

- ◆ fill an outline in different ways using Tangram pieces
- ◆ count and sort Tangram pieces
- ◆ observe how a graph shows relationships

The Activity

Introducing

- ◆ Have each pair combine all the pieces from three Tangram sets.
- ◆ Ask children to sort the pieces into groups according to size and shape, but not color.
- ◆ Invite children to describe the different kinds of Tangram pieces. Then point out that there are five different pieces, and list their names on the chalkboard in this way:

    Small Triangle —
    Medium Triangle —
    Large Triangle —
    Square —
    Parallelogram —

- ◆ Have pairs count to find how many they have of each kind of piece. Record the number they announce for each.

On Their Own

How can you make a Tan Design?

- Work with a partner. Use pieces from 3 Tangram sets to make a design in an outline like this one:

- Work together to record your work. Write how many of each kind of Tangram piece you used in your design.

- Now, talk about how you can make a different Tan Design. Make and record this design on another outline. Then write how many of each piece you used.

- Be ready to talk about how you decided on each of your Tan Designs.

The Bigger Picture

Thinking and Sharing

Tell children that you will record information about their Tan Designs by making a *graph*. Trace each of the five kinds of pieces across the top of the chalkboard. Write the heading *Names* to the left of the tracings as shown below.

Call on pairs to give the number of each kind of piece that they used to make one of their Tan Designs. Record the numbers in the graph. Then, invite these pairs to post their Tan Designs next to the graph.

Use prompts such as these to promote class discussion:

- What can you tell from the graph?
- Which pieces were used the most? Why do you think this is so? Which were used the least? Why?
- Are any Tan Designs exactly alike? Are any almost alike? Which ones?
- Which Tan Designs are very different? In what ways are they different?

Extending the Activity

Have pairs refer to the graph and try to fill the rectangle outline using the numbers and kinds of pieces used by another pair.

To make sure that both members of the group participate equally in filling the outline, you may want them to take turns placing pieces on the outline.

Where's the Mathematics?

As children create their Tan Designs, they practice filling an outline with Tangram pieces, sorting by shape, and counting. Children gain experience in problem solving as they participate in translating a concrete experience into a graphic representation. They may also begin to gain some understanding of how a graph shows relationships.

A completed graph reflecting the pieces used by several pairs might look like this:

Names	◺	◹	◸	□	▱
Jonah/Tim	2	—	4	3	—
Dara/Dan	2	1	3	1	3
Amy/Sam	4	2	2	1	3
Mike/Sara	2	4	2	—	3
Max/Curtis	4	—	4	2	—
Kate/Adam	2	2	3	1	2

As children fill the rectangle outline, some may start with large pieces and then fill in any remaining spaces with small triangles. Some pairs may try to use at least one of each kind of Tangram piece. These children may fill the outline and then make substitutions to work other kinds of pieces into it.

Children may experience many false starts. They may begin to feel successful in filling an outline, only to realize that there is no way they can completely fill it. A child might begin to fill an outline this way, for example:

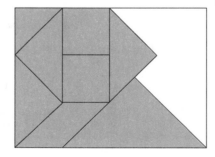

Be supportive of all children's efforts, pointing out one piece that may be substituted for another, if appropriate, so as to help allay frustration.

There are many possible ways to fill the outline. Some possibilities are shown below.

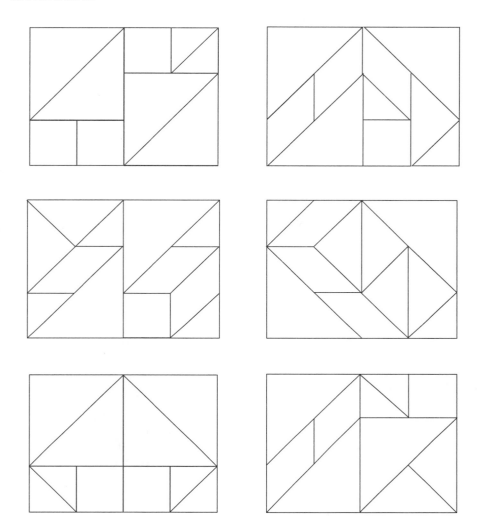

As they discuss the displayed Tan Designs, children may be surprised that there were so many different ways to cover the rectangle.

As children try to fill in the outline using the same pieces in the same numbers used by others, they may begin to understand how a graph shows relationships and leaves a permanent record of an activity.

TANGRAM FORCE-OUT

- Spatial visualization
- Congruence
- Game strategies

Getting Ready

What You'll Need

Tangrams, 2 sets of 2 different colors per pair

Tangram Force-Out game board, 1 per pair, page 97

Overhead Tangram pieces and/or *Tangram Force-Out* game board transparency (optional)

Overview

In this game for two players, children take turns placing Tangram pieces on a grid in an effort to be the one to put down the last piece. In this activity, children have the opportunity to:

- ◆ explore spatial relationships
- ◆ develop strategic thinking skills

The Activity

Some children may find it difficult to match the edges of pieces within lines on the Tangram Force-Out *game board. Help children see that one triangle fits exactly, but the other does not.*

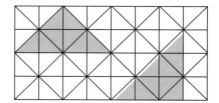

Introducing

- ◆ Give each pair one set of Tangrams and a copy of the *Tangram Force-Out* game board.
- ◆ Ask children to position two large Tangram triangles on the game board so that each fits exactly. Point out that the large triangle fits exactly when its longest side is straight across or straight up and down the game board. It does not fit exactly when its longest side is along a slanted line on the board.
- ◆ With their large triangles still in place, have children place the remaining pieces from their Tangram set somewhere on the game board so that each fits exactly.
- ◆ Tell children that they will play a game in which they try to fit all the pieces from two Tangram sets on one game board.

On Their Own

Play *Tangram Force-Out!*

Here are the rules:

1. This is game for 2 players. The object of the game is to put the last Tangram piece on the game board.

2. Each player chooses his or her color from the available Tangram sets. Players decide who will go first.

3. Players take turns placing any Tangram piece on a game board that looks like this:

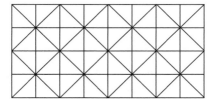

4. Each piece that is placed must fit over a number of triangle sections exactly.

5. Play continues until the last piece that can fit on the board is put down. Whoever puts down this piece wins.

- Play 3 more games of *Tangram Force-Out*. Take turns going first.

- Be ready to talk about good moves and bad moves.

The Bigger Picture

Thinking and Sharing

Invite children to talk about their games and describe some of the thinking they did.

Use prompts like these to promote class discussion:

- When it was your turn to go first, which piece did you play first? Why?

- Which pieces do you think are the easiest to place? Which are the most difficult? Why do you think so?

- Does it matter who goes first in this game? Explain.

- What are some ways to play that can help you win?

- How can looking at the pieces your partner has left help you make a good play?

- Did anyone play a game in which every piece fit on the board? If so, who put down the last piece? Which piece was it?

Writing

Ask children to list tips for playing *Tangram Force-Out*. If you have the available resources, you might ask them to record their tips on an audio cassette.

Extending the Activity

1. Ask children to play the game cooperatively, together placing as many pieces on the board as possible.

Teacher Talk

Where's the Mathematics?

The *Tangram Force-Out* game encourages the use of logical and spatial strategies. In attempting to be the last to place a Tangram piece on the board, children visualize where pieces might fit and use this knowledge to plan future moves, strategizing to deny their partner space on the grid.

As they play the game, children may notice that the game board is divided into small triangles. Some children may conclude that every Tangram piece can be made up of a number of small triangles. When combined with the fact that the game board can hold exactly two sets of Tangrams, some children may realize at the end of a game that, although there may be enough space to place the pieces they have left, the available space is not in the shape of their pieces.

As children explore the relationship between size and shape, they may develop various strategies and playing styles. After several games, some children may adopt the strategy of placing the largest Tangram pieces at the beginning of the game when there is the most space available. Other children may place smaller pieces first to break up large spaces, making it more difficult for their opponents to play large pieces.

Children may learn that certain placements can block other moves. For example, on the game board below, the two large and two medium triangles are placed so that the remaining two large triangles can never be played.

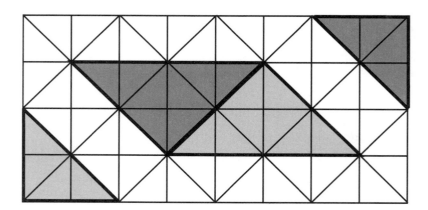

2. Have children play the game as before, but this time the player who covers the most space wins.

As children gain experience playing the game, they may develop specific strategies for winning. Some may try to place their own pieces close together. Others may scatter their pieces about the board in hopes of making it difficult for their opponent to find a good play. Some may concentrate on blocking the other player's progress, whereas others may look ahead, attempting to set up good plays for themselves.

As children work cooperatively to play the game, they may discover that there is exactly enough space to fit both sets of Tangrams. Two possible solutions are shown below.

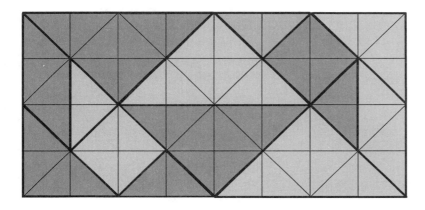

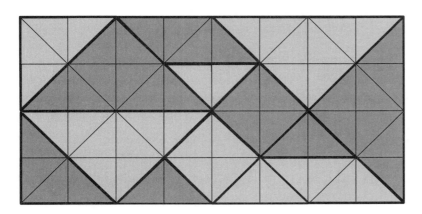

TANGRAMS MAKE CENTS

GEOMETRY • NUMBER • MEASUREMENT
- Addition
- Money
- Congruence
- Non-standard measurement
- Area

Getting Ready

What You'll Need

Tangrams, 1 set per pair

Tangram Toy Cat worksheet, 1 per pair, page 98

More Tangram Toys worksheet, 1 per pair, page 99

Small Tangram Triangles, 1 per pair, page 101 (optional)

Overhead Tangram pieces and/or Tangram Toy Cat and More Tangram Toys transparencies (optional)

Overview

Using an assigned monetary value for the small Tangram triangle, children find the cost of "toys" made up of Tangram pieces. In this activity, children have the opportunity to:

- ◆ use the small Tangram triangle as a unit of measure
- ◆ measure and compare Tangram pieces
- ◆ count by twos

The Activity

Help children see that the small triangles must cover larger pieces exactly without overlapping or going past the edge.

small triangles exactly covering the square

small triangles not covering the square exactly

Introducing

- ◆ Display a small Tangram triangle. Tell children to pretend that this triangle costs 2¢.
- ◆ Hold up a medium Tangram triangle. Ask children to think about how they can find its cost based on the cost of the small triangle.
- ◆ Invite a volunteer to give the cost of the medium triangle and to use Tangram pieces to show how he or she arrived at the answer.
- ◆ Hold up the Tangram parallelogram, square, and large triangle. Challenge groups of children to find the cost of each based on the cost of the small Tangram triangle.

On Their Own

Can you find the cost of some Tangram toys?

- Work with a partner. Use all your Tangram pieces to cover the toy cat on the outline that looks like this one:

- If the small triangle costs 2¢, which parts of the cat cost 2¢?

- Plan how to find the cost of the whole cat. Follow your plan. Write how much the toy cat costs.

- Now, use some Tangram pieces to cover the other toys on the outlines that look like these:

- Use the plan you made for the cat to find the cost of the tree, the fish, and the bird. Write the cost of each.

- Be ready to talk about how you followed your plan to find each cost.

The Bigger Picture

Thinking and Sharing

Ask pairs to identify the Tangram pieces they used to cover each part of the cat outline. Ask how much the toy cat costs. Do the same for each of the other toys. Distribute small paper triangles, if necessary, so that children can cover each toy to confirm its cost.

Use prompts such as these to promote class discussion:

- How did the cost of one small triangle help you decide on the price for the other Tangram pieces?

- After you covered an outline, how did you go about finding the cost of the toy?

- Which Tangram piece costs the most? How much does it cost? Which piece costs the least? How much does it cost?

- Which of the Tangram toys costs the most? How much does it cost? Which toy costs the least? How much does it cost?

Extending the Activity

1. Have children find the cost of each Tangram toy based on a different unit price for the small triangle, such as 5¢ or 10¢.

Where's the Mathematics?

As children find the cost of a Tangram toy based on the number of small Tangram triangles of a given value that can cover it, they explore the idea of equality and the size relationships among the Tangram pieces.

Children who are having difficulty counting the small triangles to find the total cost of a toy may benefit from first fitting small paper triangles on the covered outline, then removing the small triangles and arranging them in a line before counting. You may want to have children put two pennies on each small triangle and then count the pennies to find the total cost. For example:

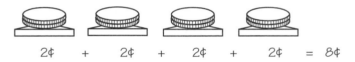

2¢ + 2¢ + 2¢ + 2¢ = 8¢

As they gain experience, some children may use their knowledge of spatial relationships to figure out the total cost of a piece without covering it. For example, when asked how much the medium triangle costs, some children may eyeball it and recognize that it is twice the size and, therefore, twice the cost of the small triangle.

As they gain an understanding of the various spatial relationships, children may also make discoveries about equality. For example, after using two small triangles to cover a parallelogram, they may decide that the cost of a parallelogram equals the cost of two small triangles. Then, when the value of the small triangle is set at 5¢, children may determine that the parallelogram costs 10¢ without having to remeasure or recount.

Tapping the pieces, holding up fingers, using small counters, and making tally marks are all possible ways to keep track of the count.

Children may use many different methods to determine the total cost of a toy. Some may decide that counting by twos is a good way to "add up" the cost. Others may count by ones while tapping each piece twice as they count. Still others may choose to add or multiply, perhaps figuring their totals mentally.

2. Suggest that children work together to make their own Tangram toy. After they record their work, have them decide on a price for the small Tangram triangle, and find the cost of their toy based on that price.

As children compare the costs of pieces, some may notice that the value of each larger piece is always an even amount regardless of the value of the small triangle. Children may also notice that pieces of different shapes can have the same value.

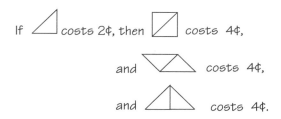

By discussing which Tangram piece costs the most and which costs the least, children may discover that the biggest piece, the large triangle, always has the greatest price no matter how much the small triangle costs.

As children experiment with different values for the small triangle, they may discover the relationship between cost and size. For example, when the value of the small triangle goes up, the cost of the other pieces goes up. If the value of small triangle goes down, the cost of the other pieces goes down.

Using values of 2¢, 5¢, and 10¢ for the small triangle, here are the relative values of the other Tangram pieces.

△	2 ¢	5 ¢	10 ¢
▱	4 ¢	10 ¢	20 ¢
◺	4 ¢	10 ¢	20 ¢
△	4 ¢	10 ¢	20 ¢
◿	8 ¢	20 ¢	40 ¢

THE GREAT TRIANGLE COVERUP

- Counting
- Comparing
- Area
- Congruence

Getting Ready

What You'll Need

Tangrams, 1 set per pair

Tape

Small Tangram Triangles,
10 per pair, page 101

Overhead Tangram pieces and
Tangram paper transparency
(optional)

Overview

Children make a shape by joining two Tangram pieces. Then they count the
number of small triangles needed to cover their new shape. In this activity,
children have the opportunity to:

- ◆ use the small Tangram triangle as a unit of measure
- ◆ compare shapes
- ◆ gain informal experience finding area

The Activity

*Help children to understand that
when they cover a shape with small
triangles, the triangles must not over-
lap or go past the edge of the shape.*

Introducing

- ◆ Hold up the Tangram square and ask children to find this piece in
  their Tangram set.
- ◆ Have children cover the square exactly with their small Tangram
  triangles, then count the triangles.
- ◆ Ask children how many triangles it took to cover the square.
- ◆ Model how children could record the square by holding it up
  against the chalkboard and having a child trace around it. Draw a
  dotted line diagonally across the square. Then indicate that it took
  two small triangles to cover the square by writing the number 2
  on it.

On Their Own

How many small Tangram triangles will it take to cover your shape?

- With a partner, choose 2 of these Tangram pieces and put them together to make a shape.

- Tape your 2 pieces together.

- One of you should hold the shape on a piece of paper. The other one should trace around the shape.

- Cover your shape exactly with small Tangram triangles.

- Count the small triangles you used. Write that number on your tracing.

- Now cut out your shape. If your shape comes apart, do the activity again. This time make a different shape.

The Bigger Picture

Thinking and Sharing

Ask children how many small triangles they needed to cover their shape. List those numbers. When there are no more responses, write the numbers in numerical order across the top of the chalkboard.

Invite pairs of children to show their shape and tape it to the board below the appropriate number. Continue this process until all the shapes have been posted.

Use prompts like these to promote class discussion:

- What do you notice about the posted shapes?

- Under which number do you see the most shapes? the least shapes?

- How many more shapes are in this column than that one?

- How do the shapes that were covered with ——— triangles compare to those covered with ——— triangles?

- Why do you think small triangles were a good covering piece?

- Do you think the Tangram square would be as good a covering piece as the small triangle? Explain.

If children question any of the postings, have them watch as you verify by covering the shape with small triangles.

Extending the Activity

1. Ask children to make a new chart by sorting their shapes according to number of sides.

2. Ask each pair of children to make shapes using any three of the Tangram pieces and repeat the activity.

Where's the Mathematics?

This activity provides children with opportunities for counting first as they cover their new shape and again when they compare the posted shapes. After children create shapes by joining two Tangram pieces, some may simply count to find the number of small triangles used to cover the shape. Others may count the number of small triangles that cover each Tangram piece and then add these numbers to find the total number of small triangles in the shape.

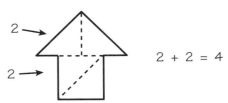

2 + 2 = 4

As children talk about the posted shapes, they must count how many shapes are in each column in order to identify which column has the most, which column has the least, and so on.

Two-piece Tangram Shapes – Covered by:		
4 small triangles	6 small triangles	8 small triangles
4	6	8
4	6	8
4	6	8

Posting their shapes also gives children the opportunity to observe similarities and differences among the shapes. For example, some shapes may look alike but actually be different in size. Others may not look alike but actually be alike, just positioned differently. (A flip or rotation can show that they are not really different.)

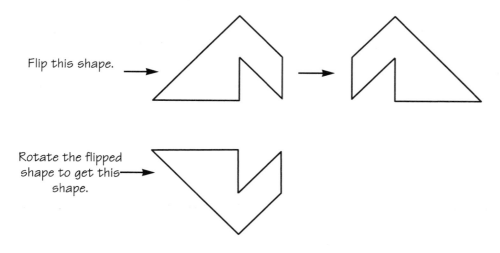

Flip this shape.

Rotate the flipped shape to get this shape.

Children may notice that some shapes that look different can be covered by the same number of triangles. Children may also observe that as shapes get bigger, it takes more triangles to cover them.

Using the small triangle as a covering unit allows children to begin to become aware that the space inside a shape can be measured, and that the procedure for measuring the inside of a shape involves using a particular unit of measure over and over again. By seeing that every Tangram piece is related to the small triangle, children begin to understand the other relationships between the sizes and shapes of the pieces in a Tangram set.

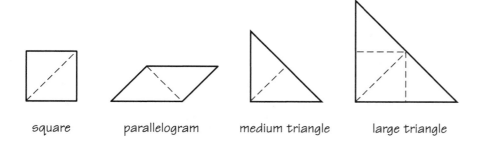

square   parallelogram   medium triangle   large triangle

TRIANGLES BIG
AND SMALL

Getting Ready

What You'll Need

Tangrams, 2 sets per pair

Tangram Paper, page 100

Scissors

Overhead Tangram pieces and/or Tangram paper transparency (optional)

Overview

Children make shapes with four large Tangram triangles, then try to make the same shape with four small triangles. In this activity, children have the opportunity to:

◆ explore the concepts of same and different

◆ begin to understand that similar figures have the same shape but not the same size

The Activity

Introducing

◆ Display two large Tangram triangles to form this shape.

◆ Ask children to identify the shape. Then challenge them to make a different square using any of the other Tangram pieces.

◆ Establish that there are several other possible squares.

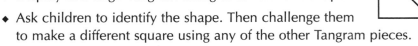

Point out that although squares may be the same size as yours, or bigger, or smaller, all squares have the same shape.

On Their Own

How can you use Tangrams pieces to make different-sized shapes that look the same?

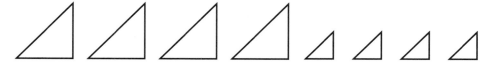

- With a partner, choose 4 large and 4 small Tangram triangles.

- One of you should make a shape with the 4 large triangles. Make sure that each piece touches part of at least 1 other piece.

- Your partner should make the same shape with the 4 small triangles.

- Record both shapes. Cut them out.

- Take turns using the large triangles, then the small triangles, to make more big and small shapes.

- Be ready to tell how your shapes are the same and how they are different.

The Bigger Picture

Thinking and Sharing

Write the headings *Big* and *Small* in two columns on the chalkboard. Invite children to show their shapes and post them in the appropriate columns.

Use prompts like these to promote class discussion:

- How are the big and small shapes the same? How are they different?
- What happens when you turn a big shape? Is it still like the small shape?
- What is the same about all the shapes you made?
- What words can you think of to compare the small shape to the big shape?
- What do you think would happen if you used other kinds of triangles? How would you compare these shapes?

Some children may decide the shapes are not the same if one is turned slightly. If this issue arises, you may want to allow children to adjust the position of these shapes to verify that they are the same.

Extending the Activity

1. Have children do the activity in reverse, first making a shape with four small triangles, then making the same shape with four large triangles.

2. Tell children that they will play a matching game with the shapes they made. Mix up the posted shapes and tape them on the board in varying positions. Have children take turns drawing chalk lines to connect each pair of similar shapes.

Where's the Mathematics?

In this activity, children have the opportunity to explore spatial relationships as they copy shapes using different scales. As they experiment with similarity, they may gain a greater understanding of the properties of triangles.

The variety of shapes that children can make using triangles may surprise them. They may notice that each Tangram triangle has two sides of the same length and one longer side. They may also recognize that each triangle has one square corner.

TANGRAM TRIANGLES

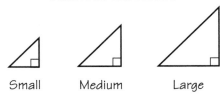

Small   Medium   Large

Children may observe that big shapes take up, or cover, more space than similar small shapes. If they trace the shapes, they may also notice that the distance around a big shape is greater than the distance around the corresponding small shape. These children are beginning to understand that similar shapes have different areas and perimeters.

While exploring the properties of a triangle (three sides and three corners, or angles), some children may recognize that there are other kinds of triangles besides the ones in the Tangram set. Challenge them to draw or find examples in the classroom of other kinds of triangles that look like these:

2 Equal Sides   No Equal Sides   3 Equal Sides
                  (no square corner)

These are some of the big and small shapes that children may make:

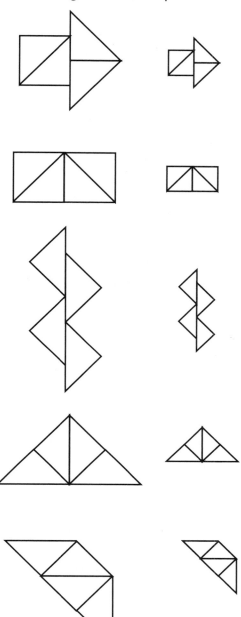

If shapes are posted at various angles, you may need to assist some children in finding different viewing positions, or turning some of the postings, in order to see a match.

WHAT'S MY RULE?

- Comparing
- Classifying
- Sorting
- Properties of geometric shapes
- Deductive reasoning

Getting Ready

What You'll Need

Tangrams, 4 sets of 4 different colors per group

Three-foot length of yarn, 1 per group

Overhead Tangram set (optional)

Overview

In this game for two to four players, children take turns making rules that identify certain Tangram pieces and guessing rules made by others. In this activity, children have the opportunity to:

◆ identify attributes of Tangram pieces

◆ communicate specific information

◆ explore the guess-and-test problem-solving strategy

The Activity

Introducing

◆ Create a twenty-piece attribute set of Tangram pieces by removing one large triangle and one small triangle from each of four Tangram sets of different colors.

◆ Display any two of the red triangles and the yellow square.

◆ Tell children that you are thinking of a rule that describes two of the pieces, but not the third piece. Ask children to think about what that rule might be.

◆ Invite a volunteer to give one rule that describes two pieces and to tell why the other piece does not fit the rule. Ask if there could be any other rule for the same two pieces.

◆ Now display the red and blue parallelograms and any blue triangle.

◆ Challenge children to think of two different rules that could describe two of the three pieces.

◆ Continue to choose other groups of three pieces from the attribute set, encouraging children to identify a rule that describes any two of the three.

On Their Own

Play *What's My Rule?*

Here are the rules.

1. This is a game for 2 to 4 players. The object of the game is to guess the rule that describes a pair of Tangram pieces.

2. Players make a large circle of yarn in the middle of the playing area. They decide who will be the first Rule Maker.

3. The Rule Maker secretly thinks of a rule that describes 2 Tangram pieces. Then he or she puts those pieces into the yarn circle.

4. The other players together choose another Tangram piece that they think might fit the rule. They put their piece into the circle.

5. If the Rule Maker says the piece *does not* fit the rule, they keep on trying other pieces.

6. If the piece *does* fit the rule, the players guess the rule. If they guess correctly, then someone else becomes Rule Maker and a new game begins.

- Continue playing *What's My Rule?* until everyone has had a chance to be Rule Maker.

- Be ready to tell how you decided which piece might fit a rule.

The Bigger Picture

Thinking and Sharing

Invite children to talk about their games and describe some of the thinking they did.

Use prompts such as these to promote class discussion:

- When you were the Rule Maker, what rules did you make?

- Did any rules have two parts? Which ones? Can you think of a way to make a rule with three parts?

- Can you always find a Tangram piece that fits a rule? Why or why not?

- What was the easiest rule to guess? the hardest?

- Was it easier to make a rule or to guess a rule? Explain.

Writing

Have children make a list of ways to compare the pieces in a Tangram set and explain how they can use these to help them in the game *What's My Rule?*

Extending the Activity

Draw two large circles on a piece of paper. Label one circle "Fits the Rule" and the other "Does Not Fit the Rule." Distribute copies, one to a group. Have children repeat the activity. This time, the children who are guessing

Where's the Mathematics?

As children think of different ways to classify Tangram pieces, they develop logical reasoning skills and build mathematical vocabulary.

When both pieces displayed by the Rule Maker are the same color or size, most children will not have any difficulty in finding another piece that belongs with them. Rule Makers may have trouble, however, forming rules about pieces that have attributes in common other than color and size.

After children have added a few pieces to a pair, they may find that none of the remaining pieces fit the rule. For example, if the Rule Maker puts down the red square and the red parallelogram for the rule *red, four-sided pieces*, no other red, four-sided pieces remain to fit the rule. As children experience these kinds of situations, they may begin to understand that knowing what does not fit is also a way to gain information about the rule.

ATTRIBUTES OF TANGRAM PIECES				
SHAPES	**COLORS**	**SIZES**	**SIDES**	**SQUARE CORNERS**
square	red	small	3 (all triangles)	1 (all triangles)
triangle	yellow	medium	4 (square and	4 (square)
parallelogram	blue	large	parallelogram)	
	green			

Children may find very creative ways to group pieces. Some may focus on the geometric attributes of objects, such as *four-sided pieces* and *pieces with a square corner*. Others may combine two or more attributes to form a set. Some children may come up with the idea of using negation as an attribute, such as *pieces that are not triangles* or *pieces that are not red*.

can place Tangram pieces in either circle to help them keep track of the
Rule Maker's responses.

The following sets demonstrate the types of rules children may use.

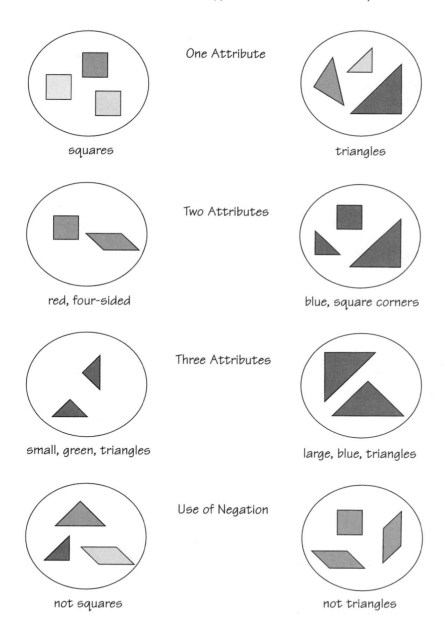

One Attribute

squares

triangles

Two Attributes

red, four-sided

blue, square corners

Three Attributes

small, green, triangles

large, blue, triangles

Use of Negation

not squares

not triangles

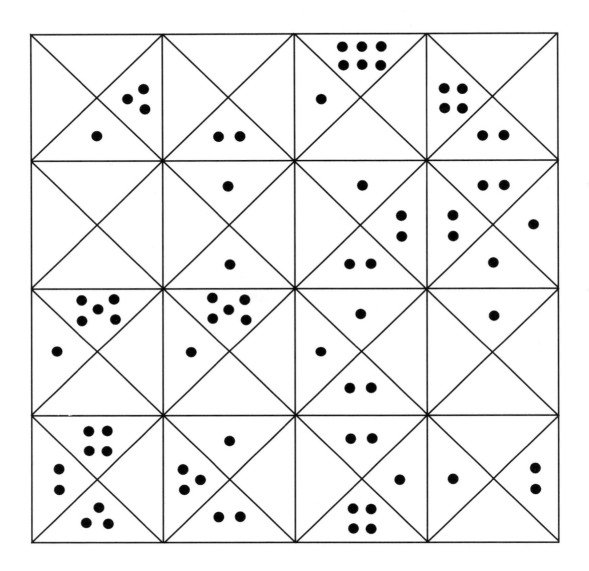

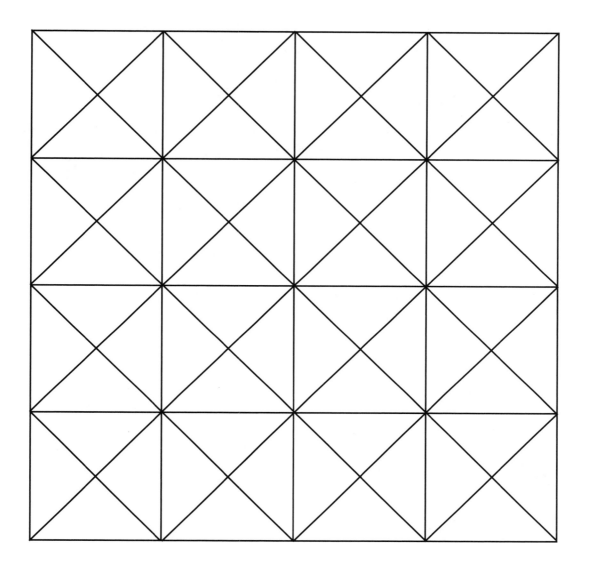

RECTANGLE RACE GAME BOARD

Tape here

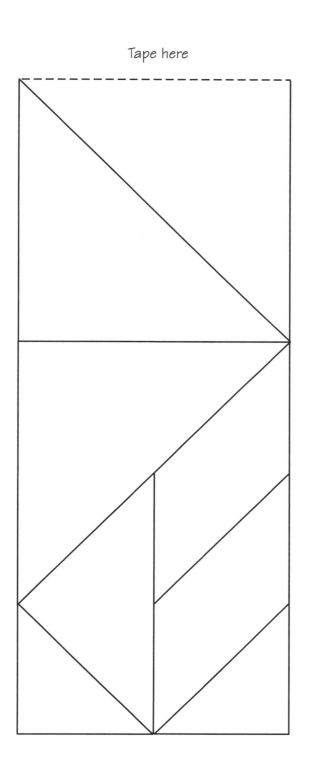

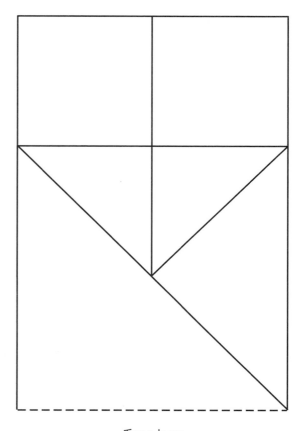

Tape here

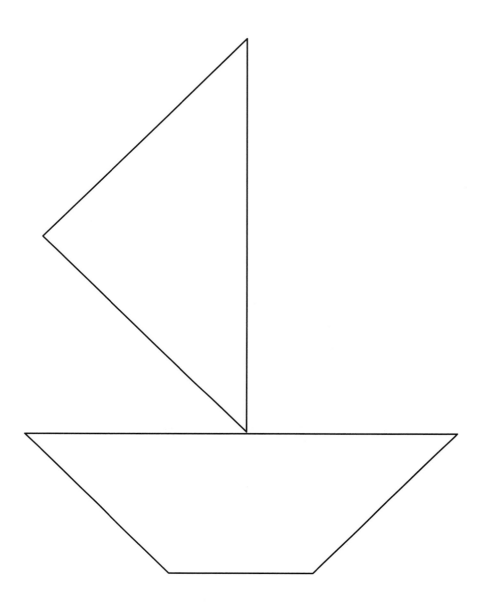

least number of pieces = _____

greatest number of pieces = _____

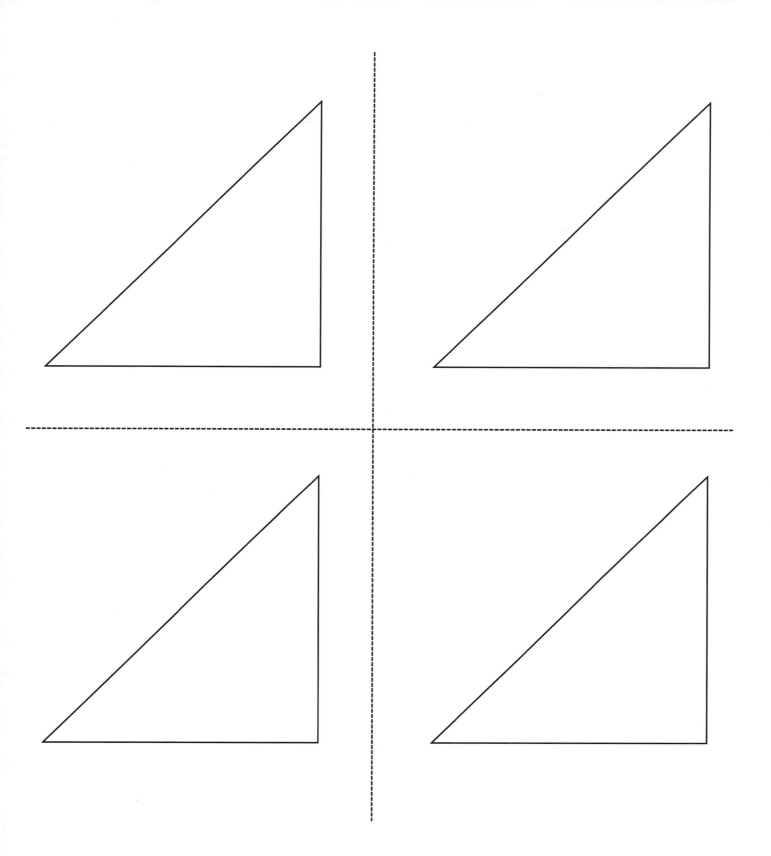

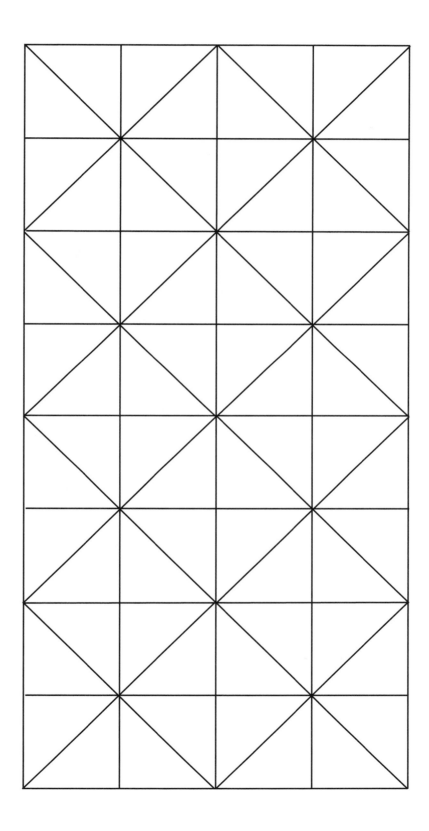

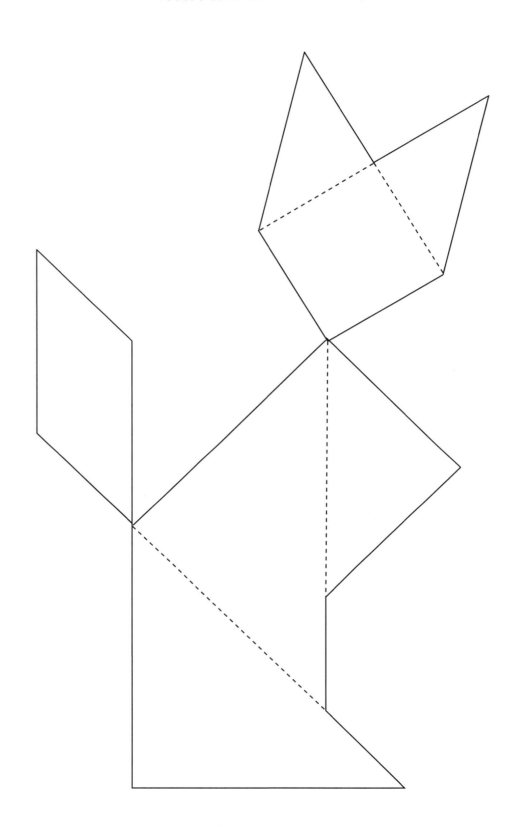

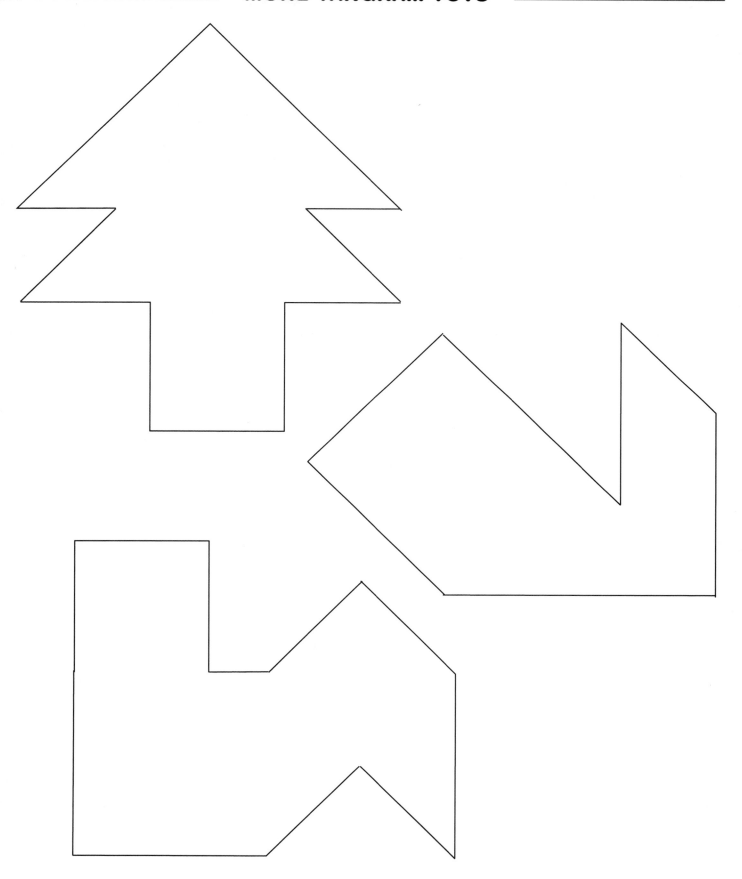

SMALL TANGRAM TRIANGLES

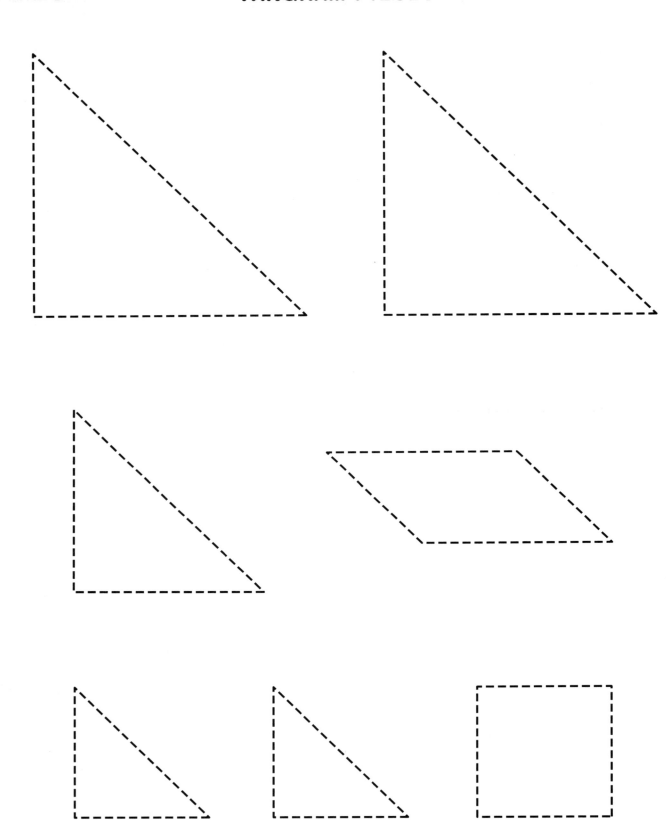

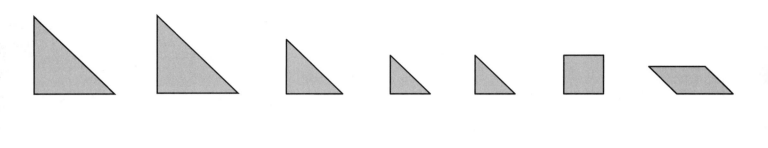

_____

_____

_____

_____

_____